Nurturing Patience
A Guide to Teaching Young Kids the Art of Waiting

Jennifer P

Copyright © 2024

All Rights Reserved

ISBN: 979-8-89409-474-8

Contents

Introduction

"Patience is not simply the ability to wait - it's how we behave while we are waiting."

- Joyce Meyer

My name is Jennifer Pham, and here I am to help you nurture patience by teaching young kids the art of waiting. Today, it's easy for little ones to get caught up in the whirlwind of instant gratification. Whether it's waiting for their turn on the playground slide or sitting quietly while dinner is being prepared, teaching kids to be patient can seem like a daunting task. But fear not! With a few simple strategies and a lot of love, you can help your children develop this crucial life skill. Together, we will explore fun activities, engaging stories, and practical tips that will make the journey of learning patience a rewarding experience for both you and your kids.

So, let's begin it with a simple example. Children move at their own speed, which often feels glacial to adults. Have you ever watched a toddler try to put on their shoes? You could eat breakfast, drink your coffee, and possibly age a year in the time it takes them to get one shoe halfway on. This book, Nurturing Patience, is all about finding humor and understanding in these moments. Because while patience might seem like a superpower, I assure you, it's a skill anyone can learn and improve—even while wrestling with a squirming child who thinks a coat is a mortal enemy.

In this book, I have targeted anyone who has ever wondered if it's possible to teach a child to wait without a meltdown, or for those who have counted to ten during a tantrum and found it surprisingly ineffective. Parents, educators, and caregivers, I'm talking to you. You are on the front lines, facing the daily whirlwind of child-rearing with a mix of dread and delight. Whether you are trying to teach your toddler the virtues of not interrupting, or you are a teacher managing a classroom where every student believes their question is the most urgent, through this book I aim to arm you with strategies that work.

I believe patience is essential in the toolkit of anyone who deals with young children, not just because it helps keep your sanity intact, but because it teaches kids how to handle their frustrations and delays—a crucial life skill.

Imagine turning a standoff over bedtime into a game that ends with everyone smiling—even you. Or transforming a grocery store meltdown into a teachable moment on the virtues of patience, without causing a scene that makes it onto social media.

In this book, I will look at everything from how to make waiting fun to how to set up your day so that patience is less required because prevention is always the best strategy. Whether you are dealing with a two-year-old who wants everything now, a classroom of first graders with more energy than a power station, or just looking to refine your ability to handle slow-moving situations, "Nurturing Patience" is your guidebook.

Remember that life is full of waiting games. You wait for your coffee to brew, for the traffic light to turn green, and yes, for that tiny human you are raising to finally put on their own shoes so you can leave the house. It seems I have spent half my life waiting in one way or another, and I bet you feel the same. It was during one such endless wait—I believe it was during a particularly long line at the grocery store as my son discovered how fun it is to unroll the entire roll of paper towels—that I realized patience wasn't just a virtue. It was a necessity, especially when dealing with children.

This realization wasn't sudden. It crept up on me, much like my decision to finally sort through the thousand photos on my phone or the slow but sure acceptance that I would never enjoy going to the gym. It came through years of practice and quite a few moments where, frankly, I lost it. Those moments weren't my finest—like when I found myself arguing with a three-year-old about why socks are essential in winter. They were instructive.

In this journey, several people have been my guideposts. First, my parents, who demonstrated

Olympic-level patience with me throughout my "experimental cooking" phase in high school. Every burnt cookie was met with applause and a quick reach for the takeout menu, a testament to their support and iron stomachs. Their endless patience during my less-than-gleaming moments taught me that love is often spelled T-I-M-E... and sometimes, T-U-M-S.

Then there were my teachers, the heroes without capes who managed not to laugh as I presented a model volcano that erupted more vinegar and regret than anything resembling lava. They patiently guided my enthusiasm, teaching me that every mistake was a step towards learning something new, even if it was just how to clean vinegar off the ceiling.

And, of course, I can't forget my own children, who challenge my patience every day and reward me with sticky handprints on my glasses and unexpected hugs that smell faintly of peanut butter. They remind me that patience is about more than just waiting; it's about seeing each moment of frustration as an opportunity for growth—both theirs and mine.

If you are reading this, maybe you're a parent, a teacher, or someone who looks after kids. Or perhaps you're just curious about how to get a toddler to wait more than a minute before diving into their birthday cake. Whatever brought you here, you are in the right spot.

From dealing with dinner-time stand-offs over veggies to handling a class full of kids who think they are all comedians, this book has something for you. Here, you will find comfort and tips on how to turn daily chaos into something close to calm. So, if you have ever been baffled by how to stay chill when your kid decides to turn the dog into an art project, or you can't find the car keys when you are already late, don't worry. I am here to help you not just keep your cool, but actually build up your patience game.

First off, I ask you to get thank-yous in order, because nobody writes a book on teaching patience to energetic kiddos without a bit of help. My family, for starters, deserves a medal—or perhaps a vacation—for living out the patience experiments that fill these pages. My kids have endured various "waiting games" that sometimes ended in giggles and other times in puzzled looks that said, "Mom, why is this fun again?" To my partner, who has mastered the art of slow-sipping coffee while a toddler narrates every single scene of their favorite cartoon, your patience is legendary.

Then there are my stellar colleagues and the professionals who didn't run for the hills when I bombarded them with questions about kids, patience, and why the two often seem like oil and water. Your insights have shaped this book into something far better than I could have managed on my own.

A special shoutout goes to my mentors, those brave souls who have mastered the zen art of not flipping out when paint gets spilled all over the new carpet. I have watched you defuse time bombs disguised as tantrums with nothing but a calm voice and an uncanny ability to distract. You are the real MVPs.

And, of course, the various organizations that contributed research and support—thank you for your dedication to making the science of patience a little less like rocket science and a bit more like a well-explained magic trick.

I have packed this book with stories (some more successful than others), strategies that range from the scientific to the slightly silly, and an honest confession here and there about times when my patience wore so thin, you could use it as tracing paper. From the great Jell-O wait to the epic saga of bedtime, you will find real-life applications of patience that don't require a PhD in child psychology to implement.

Whether you are trying to teach your little one the virtues of not interrupting, or you are hoping to finally make it through a grocery store visit without any floor-rolling theatrics, this book aims to arm you with more than just hope. Here's to less stress, more laughter, and kids who might—just might—learn to wait for that marshmallow. Or at least not eat it while you are still explaining the rules of the game.

I am the woman who could probably teach a sloth to hurry up and a toddler to wait—a feat if ever there was one! With a warm smile and an arsenal of patience, I am not just your average child psychologist. I have spent years working with families in various settings—from private practice to educational workshops, where I used plain language and real-world examples instead of baffling parents with psychological jargon.

My credibility isn't just built on my professional accolades but also on my day-to-day life, where I practice what I preach. With this book, I invite you to laugh, learn, and maybe even slow down a bit with me as your guide. So, prepare to dive into the pages of "Nurturing Patience," where the wait is definitely worth it, and the lessons linger longer than the time it takes for a toddler to tie their shoelaces. Get ready to turn those frustrating parenting moments into opportunities for growth—for you and your little ones.

So, to all who have taught me, stood by me, and waited both with and for me, thank you. This book is because of you, and for all of us who have ever secretly counted to ten—or twenty—while waiting for a small person to find their other shoe.

Be ready. This book is going to be an informative ride—with fewer bumps along the way, hopefully. While the art of teaching kids to wait can test the limits of human endurance, it's also packed with opportunities to create calm, capable young people. And who knows? You might just improve your own patience along the way.

Chapter 1: Understanding Patience

"Are you a first-time parent?" Do you remember struggling to grasp the fine threads of good parenting when someone asked you this question? Remember thinking to yourself, *yeah, parenting is one hell of a job. Why can't there be an easier way to go about this?*

Well, guess what? I was in the same boat as you. I kept asking myself, "Why has no one made an easier method, like a guide to deal with babies based on real experiences." Honestly, there is so much research about baby language, sleep routines, hygiene, and food that, eventually, all of it gets overwhelming. Most people decide to give up on it and end up making major mistakes in their child's early years.

Dearest reader, if you are a new parent, I understand what you're going through. Sometimes, you might feel burned out and frustrated. So, before we dive into the book, I want you to take five minutes and clear your mind. Take deep breaths and remember that heartwarming feeling of your child in your arms—remember the parts when you felt happy to be a parent. The first cry, the first laugh, the first talk, the first walk, there are so many memories you will cherish in your journey.

Parenting can be a bit of a rollercoaster with numerous challenges, from navigating a sea of baby products to deciphering the enigma of baby cries and mastering the art of ninja-level diaper changes.

"Do you find it difficult to figure out what your child wants?" Doesn't it sometimes feel like being handed a manual written in an alien language, and just when you think you've cracked it, they change the rules? Dialogues with a toddler often resemble a negotiation at a UN summit, with gestures, expressions, and the occasional "no" serving as the main communication tools.

But you know what? Along the way, the exhaustion of parenthood might make you miss those essential moments. I mean, what if you were too exhausted to be excited the first time your baby said something, and later, when the same baby grew into an adult and took control of their own life, you regret it? You ask yourself, "How did my baby grow up so soon? I should have spent more time with him/her when they were young." And trust me, that road of regrets is definitely a place you don't want to walk down.

But worry not, for I am here to your rescue. From learning the magical art of patience to engaging exercises to distract your baby, I have got you covered. Remember, amidst the chaos of raising a child, there is an inexplicable magic—that first word, the tiny fingers wrapped around yours, that is what makes it all worthwhile.

What is Patience?

Let us start with patience, the ability that is integral to parenthood. In its essence, it seems deceptively simple— it is the ability to endure, to wait without agitation. Yet, as I reflect and delve deeper, I'm struck by the complexity that underlies this seemingly straightforward concept.

How many times do you exclaim, "I am so done with this routine!" and "Why won't the baby just sleep?" This will sound familiar to most parents out there, and I agree because sometimes those wriggly little angels drive you crazy!

Let me share Daisy's story with you. Like most of you, she was a mother with zero experience in her first child.

Gradually losing patience, she turned into a sleep-deprived parent with a baby who seemed to have enrolled in the "Let's Keep Mom Guessing" academy.

Her problems always started during bedtime—the universal time for parents that tests our ability to remain calm. Daisy's little one seems to have decided that sleep is overrated, and the crib is more of a suggestion than a rule. That is how every night the crying began and endless rounds of "Pick Me Up, Put Me Down" ensued—a dance that we parents are normally forced to sign up for.

One night, after innumerable attempts at putting her baby to a peaceful slumber, Daisy's patience wore thin. She even considered introducing her baby to the concept of counting sheep, but of course, that, too, failed. So, there she was, pacing the room, attempting every trick in the parenting book.

Suddenly, she had an epiphany—maybe the little munchkin just needed a change of scenery. So, she embarked on a tour of the living room, inspecting every corner like baby detectives on a mission. Toys were introduced, a mini concert was performed (featuring her lullabies amidst yawns), and a few questionable dance moves were thrown in as well.

As the night stretched on, her patience faced its toughest exam yet. But here's the plot twist—in the midst of her exhausted delirium, the baby finally succumbed to the Sandman's charms. Victory! It wasn't the textbook bedtime routine, but it was an effective, unique version.

The lesson learned is that patience in parenting is not about having a foolproof plan; it is about adapting, trying everything from silly dances to improvised living room adventures, and being ready to roll with the unexpected. Sometimes, amidst the chaos, a moment of tranquility does sneak in, making the sleepless nights and mini-dramas totally worth it.

Research studies on patience suggest that it is not just a matter of temperament but a skill that can be cultivated. It involves a delicate interplay of cognitive processes and emotional control. In simpler words, you have got to juggle both your mind and heart at the same time.

Remember the tale of the Chinese bamboo tree, which lay dormant for years before shooting up in a spectacular growth spurt. The tree teaches us that patience is not about inactivity but about silent preparation, about laying the groundwork for an eventual bloom. It resonates with my own experiences when I felt stuck, not realizing that I was amid a silent transformation.

In the diary of my life, patience is a recurring theme, a steady undercurrent that shapes the narrative. Patience is not a destination but a journey—a journey that unfolds one moment at a time, where waiting becomes a canvas for growth, and endurance becomes a brushstroke on the masterpiece of life.

The intricacies of understanding the problems our kids face are a terrain laden with challenges and rewards. As I delve into these pages, my mind drifts to my own six-year-old whirlwind of energy—a source of boundless joy and occasional perplexity. This book is full of lessons I learned in raising him from an arm-length baby to a full-grown teen.

Research has told me that parents must foster a safe space for communication with their children. It is not just about being physically present but about attuning ourselves to the emotional wavelengths of our little ones. As I reflect on this, I recall instances when my son's struggles were apparent, yet the key to unlocking them lay in the realm of understanding.

My son, with his infectious laughter and insatiable curiosity, also possessed a characteristic lack of patience. That trait has, at times, tested my own understanding. My story might resonate with the anecdotes of parents navigating similar waters, and I can't help but chuckle at those shared experiences. As a parent attempting to teach their child the virtue of waiting, I was initially met with a truckload of impatience.

Then, when my son reached the age of six, he turned into an impending volcano, which was totally out of my control. He would throw tantrums and refuse to listen, even in public settings. As a parent, it was difficult to deal with his outbursts because we would mostly end up clashing like two bulls in an amphitheater.

Later, on the advice of my friends, I decided to do further research and find out how other parents had dealt with similar situations. Because, come on, I couldn't be the only one struggling with raising a headstrong child! Luckily, my research proved remarkably helpful, and I finally conquered the challenge of understanding patience.

Patience involves being able to wait calmly for something or someone, even when it is not easy. That means you have to try to be patient while understanding the problems your kids are facing. By keeping a considerate environment, parents can provide a supportive environment for their kids to grow and thrive. It's important to listen to their concerns, empathize with their struggles, and offer guidance and encouragement as they work through their difficulties.

This approach helps children feel valued, validated, and supported, setting the stage for them to develop resilience and coping skills that will serve them well throughout their lives. Patience and understanding are key components of effective parenting, and practicing these qualities can lead to stronger bonds and healthier relationships with your kids.

Numerous studies have shown the benefits of patience in parenting. For instance, a study published in the Journal of Family Psychology found that parents who exhibited higher levels of warmth, patience, and understanding had children who showed better social and emotional adjustment.

Additionally, a study conducted by researchers at Pennsylvania State University found that parental warmth and understanding during adolescence were associated with lower levels of aggression and delinquent behavior in young adulthood.

Take Sara's example. As a mother of two, she would often get frustrated when her younger son, Alex, struggled with his math homework. She would become impatient and express her disappointment, which only added to Alex's anxiety.

However, after learning about the importance of patience and understanding, she chose to approach the situation differently. Instead of losing her temper, she sat down with Alex and patiently worked through the problems with him, offering encouragement and support. Over time, Alex's confidence and performance in math improved, and their relationship grew stronger. That is how you can provide support for your children as well.

Big Challenges in a Small World

Alright, buckle up for a journey through the common rollercoaster of challenges our little humans face from infancy to adolescence. This is like a survival guide for both parents and tiny adventurers.

Infancy:

1. Sleep Struggles: Ah, the battle of bedtime. From midnight wakings to the reluctance to embrace the crib, sleep is a common hurdle in the early days.

2. Feeding Fiascos: Whether it's the picky eater stage or the chaos of introducing solids, the dining table can quickly transform into a battleground during this period.

3. Teething Troubles: Cue the tears and those tiny teeth making their grand entrance. Teething is a universal challenge, often accompanied by a chorus of wails.

4. Separation Anxiety: The heart-wrenching moment when you leave for work and your baby transforms into a clinging koala. Separation anxiety is real, my friend.

Toddlerhood:

1. Tantrum Tumult: Then comes the legendary toddler tantrums. From the grocery store to the playground, these mini meltdowns can catch you off guard.

2. Toilet Training Turmoil: The quest for potty mastery can be an adventure filled with tiny toilets, training pants, and the occasional bathroom sprint.

3. Language Learning Maze: As toddlers navigate the world of words, mispronunciations and the challenge of expressing complex feelings become part of the linguistic journey.

4. Sibling Rivalry Ruckus: With the arrival of siblings, sharing attention becomes a hot topic, leading to sibling rivalry battles.

Childhood:

1. School Stress: The transition to school brings a new set of challenges—making friends, finishing assignments, and facing academic pressures.

2. Friendship Fumbles: Friendships are like a rollercoaster, with ups and downs. Facing social dynamics and handling conflicts become part of the friendship journey.

3. Body Image Blues: Adolescence often introduces body changes and self-esteem struggles. Acceptance and building a positive body image can be a hurdle for many.

4. Peer Pressure Peaks: As kids enter the teenage realm, peer pressure takes center stage. Balancing individuality while fitting in becomes a tightrope walk.

5. Technology Tensions: The digital age brings its own challenges, from managing screen time to navigating the intricacies of online friendships and potential cyberbullying.

Adolescence:

1. Identity Crisis: Adolescence is like a journey of self-discovery, with teens grappling to define their identity and figure out where they fit in.

2. Academic Anxiety: The pressure of exams, college decisions, and the looming future can create a storm of academic stress.

3. Parent-Teen Power Struggles: The clash of wills between parents and teens is practically a rite of passage. Independence battles and boundary negotiations are the norm.

4. Mental Health Matters: Adolescents may face challenges related to mental health, from mood swings to more serious issues like anxiety and depression.

5. Substance Use Concerns: The teenage years can also introduce encounters with substances. Avoiding peer influences and making responsible choices become crucial.

This is just a glimpse into the whirlwind of challenges kids encounter on their journey to adulthood. Each child is unique, and the adventure is as diverse as the stars in the sky. What is the key? Buckle up, embrace the ride, and be that supportive sidekick for your child through the ups and downs.

Now, let us try to understand our tiny humans with a sprinkle of wisdom from Claudia Gold's book, *"The Developmental Science of Early Childhood: Clinical*

Applications of Infant Mental Health Concepts From Infancy Through Adolescence." Picture it as a parenting adventure with a dash of science.

First up, Gold reminds us that kids are like these tiny explorers steering through an uncharted territory called childhood. The book talks about tuning into their world—you know, putting on your detective hat and decoding the signals your little one is sending. It is like having a secret agent mission but with more giggles.

Imagine this: Your kiddo comes home from daycare, and instead of the usual chatter, there is a sudden silence. Gold suggests that this might be their way of saying, "Hey, something's up." So, you, being the Sherlock Holmes of parenting, start probing gently. Maybe they quarreled with a playmate or encountered the mystery of the missing crayon. Gold emphasizes the power of attentive listening, turning these moments into a heart-to-heart detective chat.

Now, let's talk brain development—Gold's expertise. According to the book, a child's brain is like a supercomputer on overdrive during those early years. It is absorbing, processing, and filing away information at a superhero speed. So, understanding their problems involves peeking into this fascinating world.

Say your kid throws a tantrum over the purple cup instead of the green one. Gold suggests it's not just about the color; it's their developing brain trying to assert control. It's like their inner superhero testing boundaries and preferences. So, instead of brushing it off, you become the sidekick, guiding them through these mini-heroic journeys.

In the book, Gold delves into the emotional landscapes of kiddos. Imagine your child clutching their stuffed bunny like it's the holy grail. According to Gold, that bunny isn't just fluff; it is a security blanket in their emotional universe. Understanding their attachment to these comfort items is like decoding a love language only they speak.

Now, communication is key. Gold suggests that even those adorable baby babbles are an intricate form of communication. It's like having your own language, where a gurgle might mean "I'm content," and a squeal could scream "I need attention!"

So, we embark on this journey of understanding—a blend of detective work, brain decoding, emotional navigation, and mastering the art of tiny talk. It's a ride filled with surprises, giggles, and a lot of "aha" moments. Because, let's face it, being a parent is like having a front-row seat to the most delightful mystery show starring your little one as the star detective.

Nurturing Realistic Expectations for Your Child's Growth

Having the right expectations for your little one is like crafting a roadmap that matches their developmental journey, sprinkled with a touch of understanding and a dash of patience. In the early days, it is crucial to anchor expectations in the realm of basic needs. Your baby is like a tiny explorer discovering the wonders of the world. Don't expect them to grasp the intricacies of a sleep schedule or the nuances of gourmet baby food. Instead, relish the simple joys of their first smiles and the magic of cuddles.

As your tiny human transitions into the toddler stage, expect the unexpected. Tantrums might become the new normal, and negotiating with a pint-sized negotiator could feel like a daily challenge. Set realistic expectations around their increasing independence, from potty training adventures to the occasional mess that accompanies their newfound enthusiasm for 'helping' with chores.

In the school years, adjust your expectations to fit their growing world. Homework battles might become a thing, and the shift from crayons to school supplies can be both exciting and daunting. Encourage their curiosity, but be ready for the occasional resistance. Remember, they are still learning the ropes of responsibility and autonomy at that stage.

Moving on to adolescence, the age of identity quests and rebellious spirits. Set expectations that acknowledge their evolving independence. Your once-chatty child might morph into a creature of few words, and the bedroom door might suddenly become a fortress of privacy. Recognize their need for autonomy while maintaining open lines of communication. Be prepared for some resistance, but also anticipate those moments of surprising maturity.

Applying Appropriate Expectations:

1. Tailor Expectations to Their Developmental Stage: Understand that each age brings its own set of challenges and milestones. Set expectations that align with their developmental capabilities, whether it is mastering new skills or facing social pressures.

2. Embrace Individual Differences: Your child is a unique star in the constellation of humanity. Place expectations that align with their temperament, strengths, and challenges. What works for one might not work for another, and that is perfectly normal.

3. Encourage Growth, Not Perfection: Instead of striving for perfection, aim for growth. Foster an environment where mistakes are viewed as learning opportunities. Your expectations should promote resilience and a healthy approach to challenges.

4. Communication is Key: Keep the lines of communication wide open. Discuss your expectations with your child, and listen to their thoughts and concerns. Collaborate on setting goals and boundaries, making them feel like active participants in their journey.

5. Celebrate Achievements, Big and Small: Recognize and celebrate their accomplishments, whether it is acing a math test or simply making their bed. Positive reinforcement goes a long way in shaping their sense of self-worth.

Remember, parenting is a dynamic dance of understanding, flexibility, and guidance. Adjust your expectations as your child grows, and revel in the joy of witnessing them unfold into the unique individuals they are meant to be. It will be a journey filled with surprises, and trust me, having the right expectations is like holding a compass to navigate the adventure together.

Chapter 2: The Science Behind Patience

Let's be honest: Patience with kids can feel like trying to herd kittens while juggling flaming bowling pins. But before you drown yourself in imaginary (or real) coffee, take a deep breath and consider this: Patience isn't just about gritting your teeth. It's actually a fascinating dance between brain development, emotional regulation, and, yes, even a little neuroscience.

So, buckle up, fellow parent/caregiver/anyone who interacts with kids, because we're about to dive into the science behind keeping your cool when faced with tiny tornados of energy (and sometimes, meltdowns).

First things first, we have to acknowledge the elephant in the room (or rather, the toddler throwing a tantrum on the floor). Your child's brain is under construction. Literally. The prefrontal cortex, responsible for impulse control and emotional regulation, is still a work in progress in your little noggins. This means waiting their turn, sharing toys, or dealing with frustration can be, well, frustrating for them.

So, when your mini-me throws a fit because you won't buy them the stuffed unicorn they already have, remember, it is not personal. They are not miniature villains trying to test your sanity; they are simply working with the tools they have (which currently resemble blunt spoons and boundless energy).

Now, enter the magic of patience. Studies show that when we respond calmly and patiently to children's meltdowns, we are not just saving our own sanity (although that is a valid perk). We are actually helping them build important life skills. Imagine their brains as neural construction sites. Every time we model patience, we are laying down bricks of self-control, emotional regulation, and problem-solving. Think of it as emotional scaffolding, helping them build the tools they need to navigate the world without resorting to meltdowns or impulsive decisions.

Patience isn't just about waiting passively. It is about active engagement. Think of it like emotional first aid. When your child is on the verge of a meltdown, validate their feelings, like having a conversation and saying, "I see you are upset about not getting the unicorn."

Offer choices, "Would you like to read a book about unicorns or build a tower with blocks?" This empowers them to feel heard and gives them a sense of control, even in a frustrating situation. And guess what? Studies show that this approach leads to fewer meltdowns in the long run, creating a win-win for everyone involved (except maybe the stuffed unicorn industry).

Now, let's address the real elephant in the room: you. Yes, you, the amazing, sleep-deprived, sometimes-frazzled adult trying to navigate this world of patience. The science is clear: even adults have emotional regulation systems that can get overloaded. That is why self-care isn't a luxury. It is a necessity. Take a deep breath, step away for a few minutes, or call a friend to vent. Remember, a patient parent is a happy parent, and a happy parent is better equipped to handle the inevitable tantrums and meltdowns.

So, the next time your child tests your patience (and let's be real, there will be many nexts), remember, you are not just keeping your cool. You are building tiny emotional skyscrapers, laying the foundation for a future filled with better self-regulation, stronger relationships, and maybe, just maybe, fewer stuffed unicorn requests (although, no guarantees there). Embrace the science, embrace the chaos, and most importantly, embrace the journey. After all, patience isn't just about surviving childhood; it's about thriving alongside it, one deep breath and giggle at a time.

Your Roadmap to Solutions

Time to dive into the pages of this chapter, which will be a guide on what to do once you have pinpointed the pesky problem. It is like unraveling the map after discovering the treasure chest. So, here is the playbook for tackling the challenges head-on.

Identifying the Problem:

First off, you have to identify the hiccup, the glitch, or the puzzle. Maybe it's a parenting mystery like decoding a sudden change in behavior or navigating a homework standoff. Whatever it is, you have nailed down the "what."

Assessing the Situation:

Now, let's put on our detective hats and assess the scene. Is this a one-time hiccup or a recurring theme? Consider the context, the environment, and the emotional temperature of the moment. It is like examining the puzzle pieces to figure out how they fit together.

Understanding the Why:

Once you have surveyed the landscape, it is time to dig into the "why." Why is this a challenge? What is fueling it? Understanding the underlying factors is like peeling back the layers of an onion—it might make you shed a tear or two, but it reveals the core issues.

Collaborative Investigation:

Make it a team effort. If you are dealing with parenting challenges, involve your partner or other caregivers. If it is a school-related issue, team up with teachers or counselors. A collaborative investigation can bring fresh perspectives and a collective brainstorming session.

Setting Realistic Goals:

Alright, you have got the lay of the land. Now, set some realistic goals. Break down the challenge into manageable steps, creating a roadmap for resolution. It is like setting GPS coordinates for your parenting journey—clear, achievable, and guiding.

Communication Magic:

Don't underestimate the power of communication. Talk to your child, partner, or whoever is involved. It is not just about expressing concerns; it's about listening, too. Engage in a dialogue, not a monologue. Sometimes, the solution emerges from the very conversation itself.

Implementing Solutions:

Now comes the action phase. Implement the solutions you have crafted. Whether it is introducing a new routine, adjusting your approach, or seeking external support, take those steps forward. Think of it as navigating the waters with a well-crafted boat—it might be a bit wobbly, but it gets you moving.

Monitoring Progress:

Keep tabs on how things unfold. Is the challenge easing, or do you need to recalibrate your approach? Monitoring progress is like having a compass to ensure you are still on the right path.

Celebrating Small Wins:

Don't forget to celebrate those small victories along the way. Whether it's a smoother bedtime routine or a homework triumph, acknowledge and celebrate the progress. It is like giving yourself a pat on the back—parenting is a journey, and every step counts.

So, there you have it—the opening notes of our chapter on what to do once you have uncovered the challenge. It's a journey of understanding, adapting, and, most importantly, embracing the process of growth and problem-solving. Onward to the next pages!

In the riveting narrative of child development, patience emerges as a steadfast companion through growth, challenges, and triumphs. As I embark on this exploration, I find myself steering across the twists and turns of my own parenting journey, guided by the wisdom bestowed by the scholars of child development.

Tools for Building Strong Patience Muscles

Child development unfolds like a delicate dance, each step revealing the unique rhythm of their growth. Patience, the unsung hero, forms the bedrock of this journey. In the early years, as the foundation is laid, it requires a serene patience akin to tending to a blossoming garden.

As infants transition from babbling to their first attempts at walking, patience takes center stage. The renowned developmental psychologist Jean Piaget would nod approvingly, acknowledging that these early milestones are not just physical accomplishments but windows into the cognitive world of the child.

The Piagetian Perspective:

In Piaget's constructivist theory, children are viewed as active learners, continuously constructing their understanding of the world. Patience becomes a prerequisite as parents observe their little ones engage in sensorimotor exploration—touching, tasting, and testing the boundaries of their surroundings.

Picture a scenario where a toddler meticulously stacks building blocks, only to joyously topple them over moments later. This seemingly repetitive act is a manifestation of their experimentation, a mini-scientist exploring cause and effect. Patience, in this instance, involves embracing the cycle of creation and destruction as the child refines their understanding.

Vygotsky's Zone of Proximal Development:

Lev Vygotsky, another luminary in the realm of child development, introduces the concept of the Zone of Proximal Development (ZPD). Here, patience transforms into a supportive structure that bridges the gap between what a child can do independently and what they can achieve with guidance.

In the ZPD, imagine a child struggling to solve a puzzle. Patience dictates that instead of providing the solution outright, a caregiver offers gentle hints, allowing the child to navigate the challenge independently. This delicate dance of support and restraint is the essence of fostering not just skill acquisition but also the confidence to tackle future endeavors.

Erikson's Psychosocial Stages:

Erik Erikson's psychosocial stages present another facet of child development, intertwining identity formation with social interactions. Patience assumes a nurturing role as children traverse the delicate balance of autonomy versus shame, trust versus mistrust, and initiative versus guilt.

Consider a preschooler determined to tie their shoelaces independently yet fumbling with the complicated loops. Patience surfaces as a guiding force, encouraging their initiative while providing the necessary support. In this context, the caregiver becomes a beacon of encouragement, fostering a sense of mastery and autonomy.

During moments of emotional turbulence—the defiant 'no' or the tearful frustration—patience assumes a soothing role. It is the gentle reassurance that emotions are valid and that the journey of self-discovery is a series of peaks and valleys. This patience is a lighthouse of emotional security, a demonstration of the unwavering support accompanying a child's exploration of their inner world.

As children metamorphose into adolescents, the landscape of patience undergoes a transformation. The adolescent years, marked by identity formation and autonomy, demand a different cadence of patience—a nuanced understanding of the push-and-pull between independence and guidance.

Imagine a teenager grappling with the complexities of self-identity. Patience, in this stage, requires parents to step back, allowing space for self-reflection and decision-making. You have to form a balance between offering support while respecting the expanding autonomy of the adolescent.

Patience is not just a passive virtue but an active force—a guiding light that supports you through the ebbs and flows of growth—a dynamic force that shapes the parent-child relationship, fostering resilience, understanding, and an enduring bond. From the foundational stages of Piaget's sensorimotor exploration to the delicate framework of Vygotsky's Zone of Proximal Development and the emotional landscapes of Erikson, patience intertwines with every milestone. As a parent, it is not just about witnessing these processes; it is about dealing with the daily complexities of a developing mind, often with a healthy dose of trial and error and a sprinkling of heartwarming stories.

Now, imagine patience as a magical toolbox. Each time you practice it, you are adding powerful tools:

The Empathy Hammer: When you patiently listen to your child's frustrations, you're using the empathy hammer to build a bridge of understanding. This helps them feel heard and validated, which, in turn, makes them more receptive to learning and cooperation.

The Frustration Filter: Remember that under-construction brain? The frustration filter helps your child navigate those big emotions without them overflowing. By staying calm and offering guidance, you are teaching them valuable coping mechanisms for life.

The Learning Lens: Patience isn't just about waiting; it is about creating opportunities for growth. When you patiently guide your child through challenges, you are equipping them with the "learning lens" to see mistakes as stepping stones, not roadblocks.

But wait, there is more! Patience isn't just good for your child. It is good for you too. Studies show that patient parents experience lower stress levels, stronger relationships with their children, and even improved physical health. So, basically, patience is like a magic potion that benefits everyone!

Of course, mastering the art of patience isn't always easy. Here are some tips to help you on your journey:

Take a deep breath (or ten!). When you feel yourself getting flustered, step away for a moment to calm down. Deep breathing exercises can be a lifesaver in these situations.

Remember, you're not alone. Every parent struggles with patience. Talk to other parents, share your experiences, and support each other.

Focus on the positive. When your child displays patience, acknowledge and celebrate it! This positive reinforcement encourages them to continue developing this valuable skill.

Make it fun! Games, stories, and even silly songs can help teach patience in a lighthearted way.

Be kind to yourself. We all have bad days. Forgive yourself when you lose your cool, and remember, progress over perfection is key.

So, the next time your little explorer tests your patience, remember you are not just keeping your cool. You are nurturing their brain, building a strong bond, and maybe even saving your own sanity. And hey, who knows, maybe you will even unlock the secret to inner peace along the way. Now, that is a superpower worth cultivating!

Let us peel back the layers and delve into the inner workings of a child's brain. Research tells us that this complex organ undergoes significant growth and rewiring during the early years. Picture it like a bustling construction site, with neurons firing like energetic workers laying down the foundation of cognitive abilities.

In the first few years, synapses, the connections between neurons, multiply at an astonishing rate. It is like a bustling city expanding its network of roads. These synapses create the pathways for communication, shaping everything from language acquisition to emotional regulation.

Now, imagine being on a road trip with your toddler. They point excitedly at a passing truck, absorbing new sights and sounds. In their brain, synapses are firing like fireworks as they process and store this information. That seemingly simple moment is a powerhouse of neural activity, contributing to their cognitive development.

As the brain matures, the prefrontal cortex, often dubbed the CEO of the brain, takes center stage. This region, responsible for decision-making, impulse control, and emotional regulation, undergoes significant development during childhood and adolescence.

Research indicates that the prefrontal cortex doesn't fully mature until early adulthood. It's like a work in progress, with the finishing touches being applied over the years. This nugget of knowledge becomes a beacon of understanding for parents navigating the stormy seas of impulsive behavior.

Impulse Control in Action

Now, let me amuse you with a tale from the trenches of parenting. Picture your six-year-old, a whirlwind of energy and curiosity, eyeing the cookie jar atop the kitchen counter. In a split second, he contemplates the daring climb, the allure of the forbidden treat tempting his adventurous spirit.

This, my friend, is the battleground of impulse control. It's the tug-of-war between the immediate desire for that cookie and the burgeoning ability to restrain the impulse. In this scenario, his prefrontal cortex is in the midst of its construction project, grappling with the decision to indulge in the cookie caper or heed the internal warnings.

You have to play the role of a supportive coach, guiding him through the process. We discuss the consequences—the potential tumble from the counter and the disappointment of breaking the rules. It is an interplay of reasoning and understanding, a moment where the seeds of impulse control are sown.

Research reinforces the pivotal role of parenting in shaping a child's impulse control. It is not just about witnessing the neural symphony from the sidelines; it's about actively participating in the orchestration. Positive parenting practices, laden with empathy and clear boundaries, contribute to the development of robust impulse control.

Jessica's anecdote will add color to this canvas. During a grocery store escapade, her child spotted a colorful array of candies strategically placed at the checkout counter. The allure was magnetic, and the impulse to grab a handful was palpable. At that moment, her role as a parent was not just to deny the request but to engage in a dialogue, fostering an understanding of delayed gratification. Let me explain this through a conversation between Jessica and Darry, her son.

With eyes wide with excitement, Darry exclaims, "Wow, Mommy! Look at all those gummies! Can I have some? Please?"

Jessica smiles tenderly at him and doesn't rush to disagree with his demand. "I see those yummy gummies too, Darry. They do look delicious!"

He nods eagerly, "They do! Can I have a pack of the red ones? And maybe some of the orange ones too?"

Jessica says, "Hmm, those sound like great choices. Before we decide, tell me something. Do you remember that special trip to the amusement park we are planning next weekend?"

Darry replies, "Oh yeah! The one with the roller coasters and the giant Ferris wheel?"

Jessica says, "Exactly! We've been saving up for it, right?"

Darry goes into some deliberation, "Yes...?"

"So, would you rather spend some of that money on candy today or save it for all the fun things we can do at the amusement park?"

The boy thinks for a while and then answers, "The amusement park! We get to ride the pirate ship and win prizes, right?"

"Absolutely! We can even get cotton candy there too. But only if we save our money now."

"But the gummies are here now..." His voice trails off as he thinks.

"I know it's tough to wait, Darry. But sometimes, waiting for something makes it even more special. Remember that time we waited all winter for Christmas, and then it was even more exciting when it finally came?"

Darry agrees with eyes shining, "Yeah, you're right! And we get to see all the cool animals at the park, too!"

"Exactly! So, how about we make a deal? Today, we can choose a fun activity to do at the park together, and next time we come to the store, we can pick out a special treat to celebrate our patience."

"Okay! Can we pick the bumper cars?" Darry asks expectantly.

Jessica chuckles, "Sounds like a plan! Now, let's go find that park brochure and start planning our adventure!"

"Yay! This wait isn't so bad after all!"

Smiling warmly, Jessica explains, "Sometimes waiting can be the sweetest part because it lets us build anticipation and appreciate the reward even more. And who knows, maybe next time we come to the store, there will be an even cooler surprise waiting for us."

This dialogue showcases Jessica's approach to delayed gratification. She avoids simply saying no and instead engages Darry in a conversation that helps him understand the concept and make his own informed decision. It also highlights the importance of positive reinforcement and offering alternatives to make waiting more palatable.

We have now discussed the concept of waiting, the joy of savoring a treat after dinner, and the satisfaction of making a thoughtful choice. It is a parenting maneuver grounded in research-backed strategies, a gentle nudge toward developing impulse control amid the tantalizing array of sweets.

Impulse Control and Emotional Regulation

Impulse control is not a solitary hero; it often partners with emotional regulation, creating a dynamic duo in the realm of child development. The ability to manage emotions contributes significantly to a child's capacity to face the twists and turns of impulses.

Research emphasizes that children who develop strong emotional regulation skills are better equipped to handle impulses. It is like providing them with an emotional toolkit, complete with strategies to cope with frustration, disappointment, and the myriad emotions that accompany decision-making.

Here's a snapshot of Janet's parenting escapades. Picture a rainy afternoon. Her five-year-old is eager to head outdoors for a playdate. The disappointment of canceling plans due to weather is palpable. This is a moment where emotional regulation intertwines with impulse control.

Moving on, we will talk about the rainy day alternatives, the joy of a board game marathon, or a creative indoor project. It is not just about quelling the immediate disappointment but about fostering resilience, an emotional skill that goes hand in hand with impulse control.

Incorporating Strategies into Everyday Parenting

Armed with insights from research and the battlefield of parenting, it is time to incorporate practical strategies into our daily arsenal. Patience, that ever-present ally, takes center stage.

1. Modeling Behavior: Children are keen observers. Modeling impulse control and emotional regulation in our own actions becomes a powerful lesson. Picture a scenario where you resist the urge to react impulsively to a challenging situation. Your child, like a sponge, will absorb this valuable lesson. Here is an example.

The printer jammed again, spitting out a crumpled mess of paper just as Janet was about to print an important presentation. Her initial reaction was to slam her fist on the desk and unleash a string of frustrated curses.

But then, she caught her daughter watching her from the doorway. Taking a deep breath, she calmly unplugged the printer, carefully unjammed the paper, and restarted the machine.

"Ugh, technology!" she said with a sigh, forcing a smile. "But don't worry, we will figure it out!"

Seeing her reaction, her daughter grabbed a stray piece of paper and started drawing a picture of a printer with a happy face. At that moment, Janet's frustration melted away, replaced by a sense of accomplishment and the quiet satisfaction of knowing that she had just modeled patience and problem-solving for her little observer.

2. Establishing Clear Expectations: Research highlights the importance of setting clear expectations. When children know the rules and consequences, it provides a framework for developing impulse control. It's not about stifling their spirit but about guiding it within boundaries.

3. Encouraging Reflection: Engage in conversations that encourage reflection. When faced with impulsive actions, discuss the situation together. What triggered the impulse, and what alternative choices could have been made? It's a dialogue that nurtures self-awareness and decision-making skills.

As they kicked the last ball of their soccer game, Sarah's heart hammered with frustration. Her team had lost, and the other team was celebrating boisterously. Anger bubbled up, and before she knew it, Sarah had shoved a rival player, sending him sprawling. The cheers died down, replaced by stunned silence. Sarah's face flushed with shame.

Later that evening, as her family nestled under a blanket reading a book, Sarah's mom gently mentioned the incident. "Honey, I want to talk about what happened at the game today," she said softly. "Can you tell me what was going on inside you when you pushed that boy?"

Sarah hesitated, then mumbled, "I was really mad we lost, and everyone else was happy."

"It's okay to be angry," her mom reassured.

"But sometimes, when we feel strong emotions, it's hard to think clearly. What other choices could you have made instead of pushing?"

Sarah thought for a moment. "I could have walked away and taken some deep breaths to calm down," she whispered.

"Exactly," her mom smiled. "Or, you could have even talked to the other team about how you felt. What would you like to do differently next time?"

Sarah snuggled closer, feeling a sense of relief wash over her. "I think I will try talking next time," she said, determined.

"Thanks for helping me understand, Mom."

This conversation, sparked by a seemingly impulsive act, becomes an opportunity for Sarah to reflect on her emotions and explore alternative choices. It is a small step toward developing self-awareness and decision-making skills that will serve her well beyond the soccer field.

4. Creating a Calm Environment: Emotional regulation is often tested in moments of heightened emotions. Create a calm and supportive environment where your child feels safe expressing their feelings. It is the emotional anchor that steadies the ship during stormy seas.

5. Celebrating Successes: Acknowledge and celebrate the triumphs, both big and small. Whether it is resisting the urge for instant gratification or dealing with a challenging emotion, every step toward enhanced impulse control deserves applause.

As the journey through a child's brain development and impulse control unfolds, it is crucial to acknowledge that this is an ongoing expedition. There is no final destination; instead, it is a continuous exploration marked by growth, setbacks, and the unwavering support of patient guidance.

Picture the same cookie jar scene that we discussed earlier. But this time, imagine your child's response after being armed with newfound impulse control strategies. This time, the internal debate is more measured, and the decision-making process is more deliberate. It is evidence of the gradual sculpting of his prefrontal cortex, the evolving interchange between neural connections, and the impact of a supportive parenting approach.

Reflection as a Compass

The first step in planning the next phase of our parenting journey is reflective introspection. Research suggests that self-reflection is a powerful tool for parents to understand their own parenting styles, strengths, and areas for growth. It is not about self-judgment but about gaining clarity on the values and goals we aspire to in our parenting role.

Armed with insights into a child's brain development and impulse control, the next step is to set developmentally appropriate goals. You need to craft a roadmap tailored to the unique needs and capabilities of your children. Research emphasizes that goals should be realistic, achievable, and aligned with the developmental stage of the child.

The environment in which a child grows plays a critical role in shaping their development. Research highlights the importance of an enriched environment that stimulates cognitive growth and emotional well-being. This is not a call for extravagant resources but a recognition of the impact of nurturing and stimulating surroundings.

Daisy's story comes to mind—the creation of a cozy reading nook in her home. Inspired by research on the benefits of literacy-rich environments, she transformed a corner into a haven of books and cushions. This simple yet intentional setup becomes a catalyst for fostering a love for reading, weaving learning seamlessly into the fabric of our daily lives.

Flexibility in Parenting Approaches

One of the key takeaways from understanding brain development is the necessity for flexibility in parenting approaches. Research suggests that adapting our strategies based on the evolving needs of our children is fundamental for effective parenting.

The image of a child's brain as a construction site isn't just a metaphor; it is a scientific reality. From birth to adolescence, this complex organ undergoes a whirlwind of development, with new neural pathways forming and connections being strengthened at an astonishing rate. Each stage brings unique needs and challenges, demanding adaptation from parents who want to nurture their children effectively.

Think of it like watering a garden. A single approach won't work for every seedling. A delicate sprout needs gentle misting, while a hardy sapling might thrive under a stronger stream. Similarly, a toddler's tantrum requires a different response than a teenager's emotional withdrawal. By attuning our parenting strategies to the ever-changing needs of our children, we provide them with the support they need to blossom into healthy, well-adjusted individuals.

This does not mean abandoning boundaries or principles. It is about recognizing that "one size fits all" doesn't apply to raising children. The key lies in remaining constant in our values while remaining flexible in our methods, like a willow tree bending with the wind yet retaining its strong core. By embracing this adaptability, we become not just parents but guides, collaborators, and fellow learners on this dynamic journey called child development.

Effective communication emerges as a cornerstone in planning the next steps. Research underscores the importance of open, honest, and age-appropriate communication with our children. It is not just conveying directives but creating a bridge for understanding, fostering a safe space for dialogue.

How do you do this? One example can be the initiation of regular family meetings. Inspired by research on the positive impact of family communication, you can establish a tradition where each member, regardless of age, has a voice. These meetings become a forum for expressing feelings, discussing plans, and collaboratively shaping the path ahead. Communication becomes the bridge that connects our individual journeys into a shared narrative.

Research echoes the significance of involving children in the decision-making process. It is not about relinquishing authority but acknowledging their growing autonomy and fostering a sense of ownership.

This collaborative approach empowers children, instilling a sense of responsibility and self-efficacy. Although it is important to realize that in premature years, children lack the experience and wisdom to make decisions on their own. So always make sure to keep a vigilant eye on their activities—let them fall and make their own mistakes, but help them pave a path that doesn't lead to future regrets.

As we plan for the next phase, adjusting expectations becomes a cornerstone. Research emphasizes the importance of aligning our expectations with the developmental stage of the child. It's not about lowering standards but about recognizing the shifting landscape and setting realistic benchmarks.

The concept of a growth mindset, popularized by researcher Carol Dweck, resonates profoundly in the context of planning the next steps. It is about fostering a mindset that embraces challenges as opportunities for growth, cultivating resilience and a love for learning.

In your parenting narrative, a major transforming tool is the introduction of the concept of 'yet'. Instead of labeling abilities as fixed, adopt phrases like "I can't do it… yet" or "I don't understand it… yet." This subtle shift in language will lay the groundwork for a growth mindset, transforming challenges into stepping stones for future accomplishments.

In parenting, understanding a child's brain development and impulse control is not just about decoding the present but crafting a roadmap for the future. It is about introspection, goal-setting, and creating environments that encourage growth. Flexibility, communication, and collaboration become valued treasures in our parenting approach. Adjusting expectations, cultivating a growth mindset, and celebrating milestones serve as guideposts along the way.

As we stand at the crossroads, let's embrace the dynamic nature of parenting, recognizing that the journey is as valuable as the destination. Through reflection, adaptation, and a deep connection with our children, we embark on the next steps, guided not by perfection but by the rich experiences that shape our shared story.

Chapter 3: Setting a Positive Example

Parents are significant models in the lives of children. They help them learn and grow, but why and how do they have such an influence? Grab a metaphorical cup of coffee, settle into your favorite chair, and let's delve into why these guiding figures wield such formidable influence in the complicated journey of parenting.

Research has painted a vivid canvas, affirming that children are keen observers who absorb behaviors, values, and attitudes from the influential figures in their lives. This, by no means, refers to just mimicry; it is a deep-rooted process of shaping their worldviews. A study by the National Institute of Child Health and Human Development delves into the impact of parental influences on child development. The findings underscore the pervasive influence of parental role modeling on the social, emotional, and cognitive development of children.

Before you rack up your brains on the kind of influence you have been making on your little one, let me tell you, it is not solely about the parents. The broader spectrum of role models, which includes teachers, family members, and community leaders, collectively shape a child's understanding of relationships, success, and resilience.

Dr. Albert Bandura's social learning theory elegantly captures this interplay, emphasizing that observational learning molds behavior. In the Bobo doll experiment, he showed children learning aggression by observing adults hitting a doll. Preschoolers who watched adults hit a Bobo doll were more likely to imitate those actions later, even if they weren't rewarded for it. This study supported his theory, demonstrating how children learn aggression through observation and imitation, with implications for understanding media violence and child development. So, conclusively, it is the lived experiences and observed actions that etch lasting imprints on the canvas of a child's psyche.

The realm of neuroscience also sheds light on the complex processes of mirror neurons. These fascinating neural messengers, discovered by researchers like Giacomo Rizzolatti, fire not only when we act but also when we witness someone else doing it. In the context of parenting, it's the neurological underpinning of children mirroring the behaviors and attitudes of their role models.

Picture this scenario: A child observes a caregiver handling stress resiliently, perhaps through healthy coping mechanisms like exercise or deep breathing. The mirror neurons kick into action, forging neural connections that encode this adaptive response. When faced with their own stressors, the child is more likely to instinctively replicate these positive coping strategies. It is a neurobiological procedure where the actions of role models compose the melody that shapes a child's emotional repertoire.

While imitation is a paramount aspect, the impact of role models extends far beyond mere mimicry. Research conducted by the Harvard Graduate School of Education delves into the concept of "invisible" or implicit learning. Children absorb not only explicit lessons but also implicit messages from their surroundings, creating a nuanced understanding of values, ethics, and social norms.

Parenting, as we know, is not a serene sail on calm waters; it is often a tumultuous journey through stormy seas. Role models, like guiding stars on a cloudy night, illuminate the way during challenging times. A study by the American Academy of Pediatrics emphasizes the role of positive parental role modeling in mitigating the impact of stress on children. When children witness their caregivers facing trials with resilience and healthy coping strategies, they are inspired to illuminate a beacon of assurance amid their life's uncertainties.

The fabric of role modeling spans generations, creating a ripple effect that binds family stories together. A study by the University of Cambridge explores the intergenerational transmission of social behaviors, emphasizing that the patterns established by role models resonate through family histories.

Let me illustrate this with a snapshot from Judy's family album. Her grandmother, a paragon of compassion, demonstrated the transformative power of kindness. Her legacy echoes in Judy's mother's nurturing approach. This, in turn, influenced Judy's interactions with her own children. Role modeling is a perfect ripple effect, where the lessons of one generation become the guiding stars for the next.

The domain of role models extends beyond the familial sphere to encompass teachers, community leaders, and influencers in a child's broader environment. A study published in the Journal of Youth and Adolescence delves into the impact of non-parental role models on adolescent well-being. The findings emphasize that positive role models beyond the home contribute significantly to a child's social and emotional development.

Diversity in role models becomes a key theme in this narrative. Research underscores the importance of exposing children to a diverse array of role models reflecting various backgrounds, professions, and perspectives. It's not a one-size-fits-all scenario but a recognition that a rich mosaic of influences contributes to a well-rounded understanding of the world.

Role of Parents and Caregivers

Let's dive into the heart of the matter: the pivotal role of parents and caregivers as positive examples for kids. Beyond the titles of mom, dad, or caregiver, we serve as living, breathing models that shape the very essence of our child's perceptions, behaviors, and values.

Lily, a whirlwind of pigtails and boundless energy, mirrored her father's every move. From his confident stride to his infectious laugh, she watched and absorbed his behaviors. Her dad wasn't perfect, mind you. He stumbled sometimes, muttered under his breath when the car wouldn't start, and even shed a tear or two during sad movies. But Lily saw not the stumbles but the way he always dusted himself off, apologized when needed, and dried his tears with a sheepish grin.

One day, Lily built a precarious tower of blocks, her brow furrowed in concentration. It toppled with a dramatic crash, tears welling up in her eyes. Dad didn't swoop in to rebuild it.

Instead, he knelt beside her, mirroring her sadness. "Oh no, that must be frustrating," he said, his voice gentle. "Building tall towers can be tricky, huh?"

Lily sniffed, nodding. Her dad didn't offer solutions; he just sat with her, silently comforting her with his presence. After a moment, Lily, inspired by his calmness, wiped her tears and started rebuilding, this time with even more determination. The tower wobbled again, but she persevered, a small smile playing on her lips. When it finally reached its peak, a triumphant giggle escaped her. This became their pattern. Dad faced challenges with honesty and humor, and Lily followed suit. She learned to navigate disappointment with grace, celebrate victories with humility, and, most importantly, know that she wasn't alone, even when things fell apart.

Lily wasn't a carbon copy of her father. She had her own fiery spirit and unique quirks. But the values he embodied, the way he traversed life's ups and downs, became the invisible threads woven into the frame of her being. He wasn't just a dad; he was a compass, silently guiding her toward becoming the best version of herself, one observation, one shared experience at a time.

Research substantiates what parents intuitively sense—we are, indeed, living blueprints for our children. A study conducted by the Journal of Marriage and Family delves into the concept of "parental embodiment," asserting that parents serve as tangible models for their children's expectations and understanding of the world.

Consider a scenario where a parent models kindness, empathy, and effective communication. It's not merely a checklist of virtues; it's a dynamic portrayal that imprints on a child's developing psyche. This research-backed understanding underscores the impact of our daily actions, forming the contours of a template from which our children draw cues on how to navigate the complexities of life.

Beyond the immediate gaze of our children, the impact of our behaviors ripples outward, touching the broader spectrum of their interactions. A study published in the Journal of Family Psychology emphasized that positive parental modeling translates into enhanced social skills and adaptive behaviors in children.

Consider a parent who exemplifies effective conflict resolution within the family. The ripple effect extends as children, witnessing these constructive interactions, absorb the underlying principles. When confronted with conflicts outside the family sphere, they are more likely to draw upon these learned skills, contributing to a positive and harmonious social environment. It's a testimony to the far-reaching implications of our actions as parents.

Authenticity is a vital concept in positive parental modeling. It's not about perfection but about genuine, honest expressions of values and behaviors that align with our core beliefs. Think of a parent who openly acknowledges mistakes, demonstrating resilience and a commitment to growth. This authenticity becomes a guiding light, fostering a climate where children feel safe to navigate their own imperfections. We, as parents, lay the groundwork for our child's understanding of integrity, honesty, and self-acceptance.

Consider a parent faced with a personal or professional setback. The response becomes a masterclass in toughness when approached with a growth mindset, an outlook that views challenges as opportunities for learning and growth. The research illuminates that children observing this mindset cultivate a similar orientation toward challenges, instilling a sense of adaptability and a love for learning.

Now, imagine a bustling preschool classroom filled with laughter, tears, and boundless curiosity. Amidst the chaos, what mattered wasn't just the children's interactions but also how their parents responded to their emotional rollercoaster. The findings, published in the esteemed Child Development journal, unveiled a fascinating link between parental playfulness and children's emotional competence.

Parents were encouraged to engage in playful interactions with their children, incorporating humor, laughter, and lightheartedness into their everyday routines. The results were remarkable. Children whose parents embraced this playful approach displayed:

Enhanced emotional recognition: They were better at identifying and labeling their own emotions as well as the emotions of others.

Improved emotion regulation: They demonstrated a greater ability to manage their emotions constructively, calming down more effectively after feeling upset.

Increased social-emotional well-being: They exhibited higher levels of happiness, engagement, and positive social interactions with peers.

The observation told us that when parents approach emotions with laughter and lightheartedness, they create a safe space for children to explore their feelings without fear of judgment. This playful environment fosters open communication, allowing children to seek guidance and build trust with their parents. Additionally, the shared joy and laughter act as emotional cues, subtly teaching children how to navigate different emotions in a healthy and positive way.

This scenario serves as a valuable reminder that parenting doesn't have to be a solemn affair. By incorporating playful interactions into their daily routines, parents can become powerful allies in their children's emotional development, fostering skills that will benefit them throughout their lives.

Consider Maya, a career-driven woman, sitting against her bedroom window, looking outside. Rain hammered against the windows, mirroring the storm brewing inside Maya. Work deadlines loomed, bills piled high, and the constant drizzle was wearing thin her already frayed nerves. Her five-year-old son, Leo, sensed the tension, his usual boundless energy replaced by a wary silence.

Maya, aware of his watchful eyes, took a deep breath. She could snap, vent her frustrations, and let the storm rage on. But then she remembered the research she'd read: children learn best through observation, not just words. So, instead of exploding, she did something different.

She knelt beside Leo, her voice calm but firm. "Baby, Mommy is feeling a little stressed today, like the rain clouds outside," she admitted, her eyes meeting his. "But that's okay. We all have bad days sometimes."

Leo's brow furrowed, concern etched on his face.

Maya continued, "What helps you feel better when you're upset?"

Leo, surprised by her honesty and invitation, thought for a moment.

"Cuddles!" he declared, his face lighting up.

Maya smiled, wrapping him in a warm embrace. As they sat together, the storm outside seemed to quieten, replaced by the gentle rhythm of her heartbeat. Slowly, Leo's worried frown softened, replaced by a contented sigh.

Later, as Maya tackled her tasks, she noticed a change in Leo. He wasn't demanding attention but quietly coloring, humming a tune. When she met his gaze, he offered a small, knowing smile. He understood. He'd seen his mother acknowledge her stress, accept it, and find comfort in connection.

The days that followed weren't perfect. There were still moments of frustration, tears, and raised voices. But now, amidst the chaos, Maya found herself reaching for the tools she'd unknowingly modeled for Leo: open communication, self-compassion, and the power of a shared hug.

Years later, as a teenager, Leo faced his own challenges. He argued with friends, felt overwhelmed by schoolwork, and sometimes slammed doors in frustration. Yet, he never shied away from expressing his emotions, knowing there was no judgment, only a listening ear and a warm embrace waiting. He had learned the language of empathy and emotional regulation not just through words but through the embodied experience of watching his mother navigate her own storms, one measured breath and gentle hug at a time.

Maya realized the drastic impact of her actions. She wasn't just a parent; she was a teacher, a guide, a silent sculptor shaping the emotional landscape of her child's life. And the most powerful lesson she'd taught him wasn't found in textbooks but in the quiet moments of shared vulnerability, where even the darkest storms could be weathered with love and understanding.

The resonance of positive parental modeling extends into the area of education and a love for learning. Research published in the Journal of Applied Developmental Psychology explores the connection between parental involvement and children's academic motivation. The findings affirm that parents who model enthusiasm for learning contribute significantly to their children's academic engagement.

Consider a parent who approaches learning with curiosity and enthusiasm. The research-backed understanding is that children exposed to this positive modeling are more likely to develop an intrinsic motivation for learning. The parental example becomes a catalyst, fostering a love for discovery and a proactive engagement with education.

As parents and caregivers, we are not flawless heroes but humans who are bound to err while raising the next generation. It's in the imperfect authenticity and the resilient response to challenges that the true power of positive parental modeling unfolds. So, let's continue this journey, not as pillars to perfection but as living examples, shaping the landscape of our children's lives with each step.

Be the Calm You Wish to See

Join me on a candid exploration of modeling patience in the daily routine of parenthood. Before we dive into the practicalities, let's peek into the science behind patience. Research from the American Psychological Association suggests that patience is not just a virtue; it's a skill that can be developed and refined. The brain, in its remarkable adaptability, can undergo changes through intentional practice, rewiring neural pathways associated with impatience.

Consider waiting—a quintessential test of patience. A parent who models calm waiting in queues or during unexpected delays provides a tangible example for children. These everyday moments become opportunities to shape neural connections, fostering a patient mindset in both parent and child.

In daily routines, patience becomes a daily practice, not a sporadic virtue reserved for special occasions. It is not a fixed trait but a malleable characteristic influenced by situational contexts and deliberate practice.

Imagine a parent juggling multiple tasks and handling interruptions with a composed demeanor. The research suggests that this intentional practice of patience in everyday scenarios contributes to the cultivation of patience as a trait. It's not about being impervious to frustration but about navigating daily challenges with a deliberate commitment to patience, setting the stage for its gradual integration into the family dynamic.

Picture a parent whose morning routine hits unexpected bumps—spilled cereal, misplaced shoes, or last-minute homework revelations. The research-backed understanding is that responding to these delays with a resilient mindset communicates to children that setbacks are a natural part of life. This modeling of resilience lays the foundation for a patient approach to navigating the ebb and flow of daily routines.

Some practical examples to incorporate into your daily lives:

Homework Hurdles and Patience

Homework—a terrain that often tests the limits of patience for both parents and children. Research from the Journal of School Psychology emphasizes the role of parental involvement and patience in fostering positive attitudes toward homework.

Consider a parent sitting down with a child struggling through math problems. The research suggests that how a parent helps with homework while maintaining a patient and supportive stance significantly influences the child's perception of academic challenges. The daily routine becomes a stage for modeling the persistence and calm problem-solving associated with patience.

Relax and Eat!

Mealtime is a daily ritual that demands almost next-level patience. It is a battlefield when our tiny munchkins refuse to swallow the food we have made. If your baby is a picky eater, you must face relentless hours of crying, burping, or vomiting on most days. Don't you sometimes wish there was an easier way out of this? Well, don't you worry anymore, because I have the best ideas!

Lily crinkled her nose, pushing the unfamiliar green blob on her plate away with a grimace. "Yucky!" she declared. "What's this slimy stuff, Mama?"

Sandy, a seasoned veteran of picky-eating battles, smiled calmly. "This, my little adventurer," she said, "is called spinach. It's like tiny green superheroes that make you strong and fast, just like your favorite cartoon character!"

Lily, ever intrigued by superheroes, peered skeptically at the spinach. Sandy didn't pressure her. She took a bite of her own broccoli, her face lighting up with exaggerated enjoyment. "Mmm, this broccoli is like little trees for your taste buds to climb!"

Lily giggled, intrigued by the analogy. Sandy continued, plating a small portion of spinach beside a familiar veggie Lily liked. "Maybe today, your brave taste buds can climb the spinach mountain alongside their broccoli friends?"

With a hesitant nod, Lily dipped her fork into the spinach, her eyes wide. She grimaced initially, but Sandy, ever the cheerleader, offered encouraging words and silly sound effects. "Is it crunchy like a superhero suit? Maybe it tastes like the magic potion they drink!"

To Sandy's delight, Lily took another bite and then another, a surprised smile slowly forming. "It's not so bad!" she exclaimed, her initial resistance replaced by curiosity.

This wasn't a one-time victory. Every meal was an adventure in Sandy's book. She offered new foods alongside familiar ones, patiently narrating their "superpowers" with playful enthusiasm. Some were met with immediate rejection, others with cautious acceptance. But through it all, Sandy remained calm and encouraging, creating a relaxed and positive atmosphere around food.

This approach resonated with Lily. She learned that exploring new foods wasn't a chore but a journey of discovery. The pressure was off, replaced by a sense of fun and experimentation. Slowly, her palate expanded, fueled by Sandy's unwavering patience and creativity.

Looking back, Sandy knew her calm demeanor at mealtimes wasn't just about getting Lily to eat her spinach. It was about fostering a healthy relationship with food, built on trust, curiosity, and the joy of shared experiences. And that, she knew, was a valuable lesson that would stay with her daughter long after she climbed her final "spinach mountain."

Technology and the Art of Waiting

In the digital age, technology introduces its own set of challenges to the daily routine, especially concerning waiting. Research from the journal Cyberpsychology, Behavior, and Social Networking explores the impact of technology-related waiting on patience levels. The findings suggest that managing technological delays with patience contributes to healthier technology habits.

Eight-year-old Ethan bounced on the sofa, eyes glued to his tablet, waiting for his favorite online game to load. The spinning icon mocked his eagerness, each revolution stretching his patience thin. Suddenly, a frustrated groan escaped his lips.

Just then, his mother, Sadie, walked in, her own phone clutched in hand. "Ugh, this video keeps buffering," she sighed, her voice laced with exasperation. Ethan's eyes darted between his tablet and his mother, mirroring her irritation.

But instead of letting the tech troubles consume her, Sadie took a deep breath. "Technology can be temperamental sometimes," she said, a playful smile replacing her frown. "It's like a grumpy toddler throwing a tantrum."

Ethan giggled, the tension easing from his shoulders. Sadie continued, "But just like with toddlers, the best way to deal with it is to stay calm. We can't force it to behave, but we can choose how we react."

She sat beside Ethan, suggesting they do some jumping jacks while they waited. As they laughed and exercised, the game finally loaded. But the lesson resonated beyond the pixels.

Throughout the week, Sadie made a conscious effort to model patience with technology. When the printer jammed, she used it as an opportunity to teach Ethan about problem-solving. When the internet went down, they pulled out board games and reveled in analog entertainment.

Gradually, Ethan's approach to tech troubles shifted. He even suggested alternative activities while waiting, showing newfound understanding and resourcefulness.

One evening, as Sadie battled a glitching video, Ethan surprised her. "Don't worry, Mom," he said, patting her shoulder. "It's just being a grumpy toddler. We can do some jumping jacks until it behaves!"

Sadie's heart swelled with pride. The slow-loading webpages and glitchy video calls might not disappear, but with this newfound skill, opportunities for connection, laughter, and learning will emerge.

Bedtime Routines are the Patience-Promoting Rituals?

Bedtime is often a battleground where exhaustion meets resistance. Research from the Journal of Pediatric Psychology emphasizes the role of bedtime routines in promoting child sleep. The findings highlight that a patient and consistent bedtime routine contributes to better sleep quality for children.

Picture a peaceful bedtime: Your child drifts to sleep, free from anxiety and meltdowns. Sounds idyllic, right? While achieving this picture-perfect scenario might seem like a dream itself, here's the good news: Patience plays a key role in establishing a positive sleep environment for your child. Here are some ways to incorporate patience into your bedtime routine, inspired by the latest research:

Model Calmness: Children are keen observers who can absorb your emotions like sponges. Take a deep breath before bedtime, even if your day went pretty hectic. Speak in soft, soothing tones, and avoid rushing through the routine. Your calm demeanor will set the tone for a peaceful night's sleep.

Embrace Predictability: Consistency is key! Establish a set bedtime routine and stick to it as much as possible. This helps your child anticipate what's coming and reduces nighttime anxiety.

Acknowledge Emotions: Validate your child's feelings, even if they seem silly. Saying, "I understand you are feeling excited, but it is time to calm down for bed," shows empathy and builds trust.

Offer Choices: Empower your child with limited choices within the routine. Let them pick a bedtime story or choose which pajamas to wear. This gives them a sense of control and reduces resistance.

Turn Waiting into a Game: Use timers with visuals to help your child understand how long they need to wait before lights out. Play calming games or sing songs while waiting, making the anticipation fun.

Be Gentle with Resistance: Tantrums or protests are part of the process. Stay calm, offer reassurance, and avoid giving in to demands that disrupt the established routine. Consistency and gentle firmness are key.

Celebrate Successes: Acknowledge and praise your child's efforts to follow the routine and be patient. A simple "I'm so proud of how calmly you waited for your story" can go a long way.

Remember, patience is a skill that takes time and practice to develop, both for you and your child. Don't get discouraged by setbacks, and celebrate even small victories. By making patience a cornerstone of your bedtime routine, you'll be creating a foundation for peaceful sleep and a happier, more well-rested child. Sweet dreams!

Cultivating Patience Through Shared Activities

Daily routines offer a canvas for shared activities, becoming fertile ground for cultivating patience through joint endeavors. Research from the Journal of Applied Developmental Psychology delves into the impact of shared parent-child activities on children's social-emotional development. The findings emphasize that engaging in shared activities promotes the development of patience and other social skills.

Consider a parent and child tackling a puzzle or engaging in a collaborative cooking session. The research-backed insight is that these shared activities, approached with a patient and cooperative mindset, become valuable opportunities for modeling and practicing patience. The joint effort in navigating challenges fosters not just the completion of the activity but the cultivation of patience as a shared virtue.

The Everyday Language of Patience

In our daily interactions, our language becomes a powerful tool for modeling patience. Research from the Journal of Child Language explores the impact of parent-child language interactions on children's language development. The findings underscore that patient and responsive language promotes positive language outcomes.

Little Lily, eyes wide with wonder, clutched a dandelion puff, its delicate seeds dancing in the breeze. "Mommy," she asked, her voice barely above a whisper, "where do the seeds go?"

Instead of launching into an explanation, Sarah, her mother, knelt down, meeting Lily's gaze with a warm smile. "That's a wonderful question, sweetie," she said, her voice gentle and patient. "Tell me, what do you think?"

Lily hesitated, pondering for a moment. "They fly away, maybe to make new dandelions?" she offered tentatively.

Sarah nodded, her eyes sparkling with encouragement. "That's a great guess! They might travel far and wide, carried by the wind, until they find a new place to grow."

Lily's face lit up. "Like little dandelion travelers!" she exclaimed, her voice now filled with excitement.

Sarah chuckled. "Exactly! And what do you think they need to grow?"

Lily thought again, biting her lip in concentration. "Sunshine and water?" she suggested.

"Yes!" Sarah beamed. "Just like us! We all need sunshine and water to grow and be healthy."

This simple conversation, filled with patient listening, open-ended questions, and encouraging responses, became a beautiful example of how parents can model effective communication in their daily interactions with their children. Here are some alternatives that illustrate this:

Instead of:

"Oh, the seeds fly away to make more dandelions." (A short answer doesn't invite further exploration)

"Yes, sunshine and water. Now go play." (Focuses on the answer, not the child's thoughts)

Try:

"Hmm, that's an interesting idea! Have you ever seen where the seeds land?" (Encourages observation and critical thinking)

"Tell me more about these dandelion travelers. What adventures do you think they have?" (Prompts imaginative storytelling)

"Absolutely! Sunshine and water are essential for everyone, big and small. Can you think of other things we need to grow?" (Connects the concept to personal experiences)

Here's how you can deal with such curiosities:

Give them time: Resist the urge to interrupt or fill silences. Let them think, gather their thoughts, and formulate their responses.

Offer encouragement: Use open-ended questions, like "What happened next?" or "Can you tell me more about that?" This shows you're genuinely interested and encourages them to elaborate.

Actively listen: Make eye contact, nod, and use facial expressions to show you're engaged. Avoid distractions and truly immerse yourself in their world.

Validate their feelings: Acknowledge their emotions, even if they seem big or small. Saying "It sounds like you're really happy/frustrated" builds trust and encourages them to express themselves freely.

Alternatives to impatient responses:

Instead of:

"Hurry up, what are you waiting for?"

"Just tell me the answer already."

"I don't have time for this right now."

Try:

"Take your time, I'm listening."

"Tell me more about what you're thinking."

"I'm here when you're ready to talk."

Beyond Words:

Remember, this practice isn't just restricted to spoken language. It's about creating a safe and supportive environment where your child feels comfortable expressing themselves. This includes:

Non-verbal communication: Use warm smiles, gentle touches, and positive body language to show your love and support.

Shared experiences: Talk about your day, read books together, and engage in activities that spark conversation and connection.

Celebrating milestones: Acknowledge their progress, no matter how small. Saying "Wow, you learned a new word!" shows you're proud of their efforts.

By incorporating these elements of patient language interaction, parents can create a nurturing environment where children feel heard, understood, and empowered to express themselves. This, in turn, fosters a love for language, builds strong communication skills, and sets the stage for a lifetime of learning and connection. Remember, the conversation is a dance, and patience is the key to unlocking its full potential.

Walking the Talk

Let's dive into a down-to-earth conversation about the importance of walking the talk when it comes to parenting.

Picture a parent who extols the virtues of kindness but, when cut off in traffic, reacts with frustration. The research-backed understanding is that the child witnessing this incongruence is more likely to absorb the actual behavior rather than the preached value.

Actions Echo Louder Than Words

When parents say one thing and do another, it creates confusion for children and weakens the impact of verbal instructions.

Delena was excited for movie night, a weekly ritual she cherished. But lately, something felt off. Dad, champion of "limiting screen time," seemed glued to his own phone even more than usual.

"Delena, remember, screen time needs to be limited," he said, his eyes glued to the glowing rectangle in his hand. "It's important to make time for other activities."

Delena frowned. Dad's words felt hollow, echoing against the rhythmic tap-tap-tap of his thumbs. She longed to curl up with him on the couch, lost in the fantastical world of their chosen movie, but his divided attention left her feeling adrift.

The movie night unfolded in a similar vein. Between mumbled comments about emails and sporadic swipes, Dad offered half-hearted attempts at engagement. Delena, feeling unheard and unseen, retreated into her own silent world, scrolling through her own device.

Mealtimes became silent battles for his attention, punctuated by frustrated sighs and exasperated glances at his ever-present phone. Delena's own screen time increased, a reflection of the disconnect she felt.

One evening, as the silence stretched around them, Delena finally broke. "Dad," she said, her voice small but firm, "you say screen time is bad, but how come you're always on your phone?"

The question hung heavy in the air. Dad, finally meeting her gaze, saw the hurt and confusion reflected in his daughter's eyes. The realization hit him like a tidal wave. His actions, louder than any words, were sending a mixed message, undermining the very values he tried to instill.

That night, a shift began. Phones were put away during family time. Conversations flowed, punctuated by genuine laughter and shared experiences. Movie nights became truly shared, filled with whispered commentary and popcorn battles.

Old habits die hard, and temptations lurked. But Dad rebuilt the bridge of trust. He learned that actions truly do speak louder than words and that in the tapestry of parenting, consistency was the thread that wove love and understanding.

Teaching Responsibility Through Action:

Responsibility is a value often instilled through actions rather than words alone.

Imagine two siblings, Maya and Ethan, both teenagers, navigating the tricky terrain of growing up. Both parents value responsibility, but their approaches differ starkly.

The Talking Track: Mr. and Mrs. Miller rely heavily on lectures. "Clean your room!" they'd often bark, followed by reminders and repeated nagging. While Misa diligently checked tasks off her list, Iran, frustrated by the constant harping, often procrastinated, leading to arguments and resentment.

The Action Arena: Meanwhile, Mr. and Mrs. Miller embodied responsibility through their daily lives. They paid bills promptly, volunteered at the local library, and openly discussed financial decisions with their children. Misa and Iran observed, absorbed, and began taking initiative. Iran helped with yard work without prompting, and Misa started managing her allowance responsibly.

This scenario reflects the key finding of a study published in the Journal of Child Development: Children learn responsibility primarily through observing and imitating parental behavior, not just verbal instructions.

Helpful Insights:

Modeling Matters: Children are sharp observers, mimicking parents' actions more readily than internalizing lectures. Seeing parents follow through on commitments, manage time effectively, and take responsibility for their mistakes becomes a powerful learning experience.

Shared Ownership: Involve children in age-appropriate responsibilities within the household. Instead of dictating chores, create a collaborative "family to-do list" and assign tasks based on interests and abilities. This fosters a sense of ownership and encourages initiative.

Open Communication: Talk openly about your own struggles with responsibility, highlighting how you manage them. This creates a safe space for children to share their own challenges and seek guidance without judgment.

Natural Consequences: Allow children to experience the natural consequences of their actions. If they forget homework, let them face the teacher's reprimand. This teaches them accountability and encourages them to plan better next time.

By shifting the focus from telling to showing, parents can create an environment where responsibility flourishes naturally. Remember, actions speak louder than words, and the values we embody become the lessons our children carry forward.

Fostering Empathy in Daily Interactions:

Empathy, a cornerstone of healthy relationships, is best cultivated through empathetic actions. Research from the Journal of Genetic Psychology explores the role of parental modeling in the development of empathy in children. The findings suggest that parents who actively demonstrate empathy in their daily interactions contribute significantly to the nurturing of this crucial social skill.

Consider a parent responding with empathy when a friend shares a challenge. The children, witnessing this empathetic response, learn not just the words but the lived experience of empathy. It's about creating a ripple effect where the empathetic actions of parents become the guiding stars for children navigating their own social landscapes.

Building Trust Through Consistency

Trust, a foundational element in parent-child relationships, is intricately linked to the consistency between words and actions. Research published in the prestigious Child Development journal delves into the fascinating world of parental consistency and its impact on children's emotional well-being.

Just like bricks need mortar to form a sturdy structure, children require consistency in their environment to build a strong sense of trust. This study highlights that parents who exhibit alignment between their words and actions act as the "emotional mortar," solidifying the foundation of trust and security in their children.

Picture a parent promising to attend a school event and consistently following through. The research-backed insight is that this consistency builds a foundation of trust, reinforcing the reliability of parental words. It's not just about making promises; it's about honoring them through actions, creating a secure space where children can trust the words spoken by their parents.

By aligning their actions with their words, parents can act as builders of trust. Here's how:

Follow through on promises: If you say "yes" to playtime, make sure it happens. Consistency builds trust and teaches children they can rely on your word.

Model the behavior you expect: Want your child to be patient? Show them patience in your own interactions. Children learn by observing, and your actions speak louder than words.

Apologize for mistakes: We all make them! Taking ownership and apologizing for missteps shows your child you're human and builds trust that they can be honest too.

Embrace open communication: Explain your actions when necessary, creating a space for dialogue and understanding.

Remember, building trust is a journey, not a destination. There will be bumps along the way, but by striving for consistency and being mindful of the impact of your actions, you can become the builder of a secure and trusting environment for your child, one brick (and mortar!) at a time.

Addressing Conflict with Constructive Modeling

Conflict is an inevitable part of human interactions, and how parents navigate conflict greatly influences children's conflict-resolution skills. While parental conflict resolution is certainly significant, research published in Child Development sheds light on another crucial aspect: parental emotional regulation. The study suggests that children learn to manage their own emotions not just through explicit instruction but by observing and absorbing their parents' behavior.

This study highlights the profound impact of modeling emotional regulation. Through their everyday interactions, parents become silent teachers, shaping their children's emotional landscape. Here are some key takeaways:

Acknowledge emotions: Validate your child's feelings, even negative ones. Show them that it's okay to feel upset, disappointed, or angry.

Model coping mechanisms: Show them healthy ways to manage their emotions, like deep breathing, relaxation techniques, or expressing feelings constructively.

Talk about your own experiences: Share how you deal with your own emotions, providing context and understanding for their struggles.

Focus on problem-solving: Guide them toward solutions instead of dwelling on negativity. Teach them communication skills and conflict-resolution strategies.

Remember, children are keen observers. While direct instruction is important, the unspoken language of your emotional regulation holds immense power. By modeling healthy coping mechanisms and acknowledging their feelings, you equip them with valuable tools to navigate their own emotional storms, fostering resilience and emotional intelligence that will benefit them throughout their lives.

Imagine a parent addressing a disagreement with a partner through open communication and compromise. The research-backed understanding is that children witnessing these constructive conflict resolution behaviors learn valuable lessons in navigating differences. It's not about avoiding conflict but about modeling effective ways to address and resolve it, equipping children with essential life skills.

Cultivating a Positive Self-Image

Parental actions play a pivotal role in shaping children's self-perception. Research in the Journal of Child and Family Studies reveals a powerful truth: Our children learn about self-worth not just from our words but also from our actions. By modeling positive self-image behaviors, we can nurture their self-esteem, building a foundation for confidence and emotional well-being. Here are some key takeaways and actionable advice inspired by the study:

Embrace Self-Compassion

Model acceptance: Talk openly about your own imperfections and challenges. Show yourself grace and kindness, even when you make mistakes.

Practice self-care: Make time for activities that nourish your physical and emotional well-being. Let your child see you prioritizing your own needs.

Challenge negative self-talk: Be mindful of your internal dialogue and avoid criticizing yourself in front of your child. Replace negativity with self-acceptance and positive affirmations.

Celebrate Strengths and Effort

Focus on growth, not perfection: Recognize and praise your child's effort and progress, not just the final outcome. Celebrate their unique strengths and talents.

Offer constructive feedback: When necessary, focus on specific behaviors and offer guidance for improvement. Avoid personal attacks or harsh criticism.

Encourage healthy challenges: Let your child try new things and experience setbacks. Use these opportunities to teach them resilience and the importance of trying again.

Promote Body Positivity

Model acceptance of your own body: Avoid negative self-talk about your appearance and promote healthy body image through your actions and conversations.

Focus on health and well-being: Frame discussions about food and exercise around health and feeling good rather than aesthetics or weight control.

Celebrate diversity: Appreciate and celebrate the different shapes, sizes, and abilities of people around you. Help your child develop a positive view of their own unique body.

Remember;

Consistency is key: These behaviors need to be modeled consistently for maximum impact. Be patient and understanding with yourself and your child.

Open communication: Create a safe space for your child to talk about their feelings and struggles related to self-esteem. Listen actively and offer support without judgment.

Seek professional help: If you have concerns about your child's self-esteem, don't hesitate to seek professional advice from a therapist or counselor.

By incorporating these tips into your everyday life, you can become a powerful role model, fostering a healthy self-image in your child and equipping them with the confidence to thrive in life. Remember, your positive self-image journey impacts not just you but also the incredible little learners watching and absorbing every step of the way.

The Pitfalls of Incongruence

Incongruence between words and actions can lead to unintended consequences. A study published in the journal Psychological Science highlights the impact of parental hypocrisy on adolescents' attitudes and behaviors. The findings suggest that adolescents are more likely to rebel against instructions perceived as hypocritical, emphasizing the need for alignment between what parents say and do.

Picture a scenario where a parent advises their child to prioritize outdoor activities while consistently opting for screen time themselves. The research-backed understanding is that this incongruence can lead to resistance and rebellion, as adolescents are quick to detect disparities between parental instructions and actions. It's a reminder that authenticity and consistency are key components of effective parenting.

As we navigate the intricacies of parenting, let's remember that our actions speak louder than words. Research paints a vivid picture of the impact parental modeling has on children's behavior, values, and social skills. From emotional intelligence to responsibility, from empathy to trust, parenting is woven through the lived experiences and actions of parents.

So, as you guide your children through the maze of life, remember that being the example is not just a parental duty; it's a gift. It's about creating a legacy of values and behaviors that extend beyond the spoken instructions. It's about showing, not just telling, because, in the everyday actions of parenthood, the echo of your example becomes the guiding melody in your children's lives.

Chapter 4: Creating a Patient Environment

Forget the tantrums, the endless questions, and the sticky-fingered messes. Imagine a world where parenting feels like a gentle breeze instead of a hurricane—a world where patience isn't just something you *should* have but something that effortlessly flows from your fingertips like magic dust.

Ditch the gritted teeth and strained smiles, grab your metaphorical paintbrush, and let's paint a picture of peace, understanding, and connection. This chapter isn't just about parenting—it's about rediscovering the joy in the journey, one patient breath at a time. Are you ready?

In the fast-paced rhythm of modern living, cultivating patience becomes not just a choice but a deliberate practice, an intentional way of being within the family dynamic. This isn't about imposing an idealized version of patience; it's about acknowledging the messy, unpredictable journey of parenthood and infusing it with the calming hue of patience.

As we begin this journey, let's consider the role of research that underscores the significance of a patient environment. According to a study by Eisenberg et al., "The Cascading Effects of Parental Patience on Child Emotional Regulation" (2014), children of more patient parents displayed better emotion regulation skills. They were calmer, more adaptable to challenging situations, and less likely to experience intense negative emotions.

When parents remained calm and understanding during child meltdowns, it helped de-escalate the situation and allowed the child to calm down more quickly. This created a positive feedback loop, fostering better emotional regulation in both parent and child.

The benefits of parental patience extended beyond immediate interactions. Children of patient parents showed better emotional regulation skills in other contexts, such as at school or with peers. Eisenberg's research provided concrete evidence that cultivating a patient environment within the family isn't just about avoiding tantrums but about supporting children's overall emotional well-being and development.

Patience isn't just an individual trait; it's a communal force that sets the tone for the entire household. When parents actively cultivate and model patience, it creates a ripple effect, influencing the family dynamics in profound ways.

Imagine a scenario where a parent responds to a child's curiosity with unhurried explanations and gentle guidance. These small, patient interactions contribute to a positive family culture, fostering an environment where learning, growth, and emotional well-being can flourish.

In the ebb and flow of family life, challenges are inevitable. However, a patient environment serves as a breeding ground for emotional resilience. Studies by Kristin A. Gottman and John Gottman, the founders of The Gottman Institute, found that couples who practiced active listening, effective communication, and emotional regulation (key components of a patient environment) had children who displayed:

Higher levels of Emotional Intelligence: These children were better at understanding and managing their own emotions and those of others. They were also more likely to develop adaptive coping mechanisms when faced with setbacks or disappointments.

Improved social skills: They formed stronger friendships and faced social situations with greater ease.

Reduced anxiety and depression: They were less likely to experience mental health challenges.

Stronger academic performance: They tended to achieve higher grades and perform better in school.

Consider a parent dealing with a toddler's tantrum with understanding rather than frustration. These patient responses contribute to the emotional resilience of children, teaching them that challenges are a natural part of life and can be conquered with composure and grace.

Effective Communication as the Bedrock

Communication is the heartbeat of any family, and a patient environment becomes the fertile ground for effective and meaningful interactions. Patience in communication leads to better understanding, increased empathy, and strengthened bonds within the family unit.

A parent should actively listen to a teenager's concerns without rushing to provide solutions. Patient communication patterns foster a sense of validation and openness, creating a space where family members feel heard and understood.

Shaping Positive Behavior Modeling

Parents are the primary influencers in a child's life, and the way they model behavior sets the stage for the child's own actions. A patient environment isn't just about avoiding frustration; it's about actively demonstrating constructive ways to navigate challenges.

Research by Graziano et al. in the study "The Socialization of Patience in Early Childhood" (2019) suggests that children are more likely to emulate patient behaviors when they see them consistently modeled by their parents. This suggests that creating a patient environment can help children develop the important skill of being enduring.

Creating Time for Connection

In the hustle and bustle of daily life, time often becomes a precious commodity. However, a patient environment prioritizes quality over quantity. Spending unhurried, focused time with family members fosters deeper connections and strengthens the emotional bonds within the family.

So set aside time for your child, where you put aside all distractions and actively engage in a leisurely conversation. Such moments of patient connection contribute to a sense of security and belonging, creating a family environment where your kid will feel valued and understood. It will also build a sense of trust in your child, and they will feel comfortable opening up to you.

According to a study, "The Longitudinal Study of Parent-Child Conversations" by Alan Booth and Ann Crouter (2003), children who had frequent and positive conversations with their parents were characterized by:

Active listening: Parents truly listen and respond to their children's ideas and feelings.

Emotional warmth: Conversations filled with affection, encouragement, and support.

Patience and understanding: Parents allow children to express themselves without judgment or interruption.

Demonstrated:

Stronger emotional well-being: These children experienced lower levels of anxiety and depression.

Improved social skills: They developed better communication and conflict-resolution skills.

Higher academic achievement: They tended to perform better in school.

Stronger parent-child bond: The children felt closer to their parents and more comfortable confiding in them.

This study focuses on positive parent-child communication and suggests that setting aside time for patient, engaged conversations can significantly impact children's development and well-being. It's not just about talking; it's about creating a safe space for genuine connection and understanding, fostering a sense of security and belonging that empowers children to thrive.

Technological Challenges

In the digital age, technology introduces its own set of challenges to family life. A patient environment acknowledges these challenges and approaches them with a balanced and patient mindset. Families who actively develop patience in dealing with technology-related issues create healthier digital habits.

Richard watched as Ron's eyes glued themselves to the tablet screen, fingers tapping furiously through a game. A part of him wanted to yank the device away and impose another screen time limit. But Richard knew that wouldn't solve anything. Instead, he settled down beside his son, a soft smile on his face.

"Mind if I join the adventure?" he asked, peering at the screen.

Ron's eyes flickered up, surprise momentarily chasing away the hypnotic glow. "Uh, are you sure, Dad?"

Richard took the tablet gingerly, not taking control but mirroring Ron's actions. He pointed out hidden details and the strategic value of specific moves and even suggested alternative approaches. The tension in Ron's shoulders, usually present during these gaming sessions, began to melt away.

"Did you ever play games like this when you were young?" Ron asked, curiosity breaking through his usual gaming silence.

Richard chuckled, "Not quite like this, but we had our own adventures! We built forts, played hide-and-seek, and explored the neighborhood like it was a jungle."

Intrigued, Ron put down the tablet completely. "Really? Can you tell me about them?"

And so, the conversation shifted. Richard didn't lecture about screen time limits. He didn't preach about the evils of technology. Instead, he shared his own experiences, fostering a connection that transcended the digital divide. He showed Ron the possibilities beyond the screen, the adventures waiting just outside their door.

The next day, after school, Richard found Ron in the backyard, constructing a makeshift fort out of sheets and branches. A book lay open beside him, filled with images of medieval castles. The tablet? It had been abandoned on the table, forgotten.

Later that evening, snuggled under the covers, Richard read Ron a story about knights and dragons.

As he finished the chapter, Ron looked up, eyes shining.

"Can we play together tomorrow? Like knights searching for treasure?"

Richard smiled, his heart lighter than it had been in weeks. "Absolutely," he said, "But first, how about we set a time limit on the tablet so we can have enough energy for our adventure?"

This time, the suggestion came not from a frustrated parent but from a partner or friend, laying the foundation for a positive relationship with technology built on trust, understanding, and shared experiences. And the journey had just begun.

How Environments Shape Young Minds?

Picture a young mind as a delicate, impressionable canvas eagerly absorbing the colors and textures of the world around it. The environment in which children are raised acts as a powerful sculptor, shaping their cognitive, emotional, and social landscapes. The concept is not merely about the physical space but extends to the emotional climate within the family—a dynamic interplay that significantly influences a child's formative years.

Physical Environment

The spaces where children live, play, and learn become the backdrop for their early experiences. The physical environment can impact cognitive development, attention span, and overall well-being in children.

Research by Dianne A. Vella-Brodrick & Krystyna Gilowska on the "Effects of Nature (Greenspace) on Cognitive Functioning in School Children and Adolescents: a Systematic Review" (2022) provided compelling evidence suggesting that exposure to nature can positively impact cognitive functioning in young people. Here's an overview of its key findings:

Attention: Children in greener environments displayed better attention spans and reduced distractibility.

Memory: Studies suggested enhanced memory performance and recall after spending time in nature.

Executive Function: Greener environments were associated with improved cognitive flexibility, decision-making, and problem-solving skills.

Stress and Well-being: Exposure to nature was linked to reduced stress levels and increased overall well-being, which can indirectly improve cognitive function.

Children exposed to greenspace displayed improved performance in tasks assessing memory, attention, information processing, and executive function.

The review presented promising evidence that incorporating more nature experiences into children's lives, particularly in educational settings, enhanced their cognitive development and learning potential.

Imagine your child's eyes lighting up as they explore a room filled with colorful shapes, engaging textures, and natural elements. Carefully curated environments can work wonders in boosting their cognitive development and creativity, while cluttered or chaotic spaces can hinder concentration and create unnecessary stress.

The Science of Stimulation

Studies like "The Impact of the Physical Environment on Preschool Children's Play and Learning" (2015) reveal the positive impact of well-designed spaces. Children in environments with diverse textures, colors, and natural materials displayed increased:

Cognitive development: Improved problem-solving, memory, and critical thinking skills.

Creativity and imagination: Enhanced ability to engage in imaginative play and explore new ideas.

Focus and concentration: Reduced distractions and ability to stay engaged in tasks.

Emotional well-being: Feelings of calm, security, and a sense of belonging.

Declutter for Clarity

On the other hand, cluttered or chaotic spaces can have the opposite effect. Research published in "Environmental Psychology" (2013) found that cluttered environments can:

1. Increase stress and anxiety in children.

2. Hinder their ability to focus and concentrate.

3. Limit their opportunities for exploration and imaginative play.

Tips for a Stimulating Space

Embrace natural elements: Bring in plants, sunlight, and natural materials like wood and stone. Offer a variety of textures and materials to engage their senses. Include soft fabrics, smooth wood, and stimulating shapes in their play area. Consider incorporating natural elements like rocks, water, and sand for an extra boost.

Use color strategically: Surround your child with a stimulating yet calming color palette. Warm colors like yellows and oranges can ignite creativity, while cool tones like blues and greens promote focus and relaxation. Opt for a balance, avoiding overwhelming bright shades.

Provide open-ended toys: Instead of toys with predetermined functions, provide open-ended ones that encourage imagination and exploration. Blocks, building sets, art supplies, and dress-up clothes ignite creativity and problem-solving skills.

Create designated areas: Dedicate spaces for different activities, like reading, building, and imaginative play. Make sure to also make separate spaces for quiet time and relaxation. Include soft blankets, pillows, and their favorite books to create a safe haven where they can de-stress and recharge.

Declutter regularly: A visually cluttered environment can be overwhelming for young minds. Regularly declutter your child's play area, keeping only toys they actively use. This creates a calmer space and helps them focus on their explorations.

Remember, the ideal environment is unique to each child. Observe what sparks their curiosity and adjust accordingly. By creating a nurturing space that stimulates exploration and imagination, you're giving your child a valuable gift, the foundation for lifelong learning and creativity.

Bonus Tip: Engage your child in the design process. Let them choose colors, arrange their toys, and add personal touches. This fosters ownership and creates a space they truly connect with.

Emotional Climate

Beyond the tangible, the emotional climate within the family becomes the unseen force shaping a child's emotional intelligence and social skills.

In her renowned study, "Parenting Styles and Children's Emotional Adjustment" (2018), Diana Baumrind identified four main parenting styles based on two key dimensions: parental responsiveness (warmth, affection) and parental demandingness (rules, expectations). Here's a deeper dive into the key findings and how they relate to children's emotional adjustment:

1. Authoritative Parenting: This refers to higher responsiveness and high demandingness. These parents are warm, nurturing, and responsive to their children's needs while also setting clear expectations and enforcing reasonable rules. They provide guidance and support but encourage autonomy and independence.

Children raised by authoritative parents tend to have:

- Higher self-esteem and confidence

- Stronger social skills and empathy

- Better emotional regulation and coping skills

- Lower levels of anxiety and depression

2. Authoritarian Parenting: This refers to low responsiveness and high demandingness. These parents are strict and demanding, setting and enforcing rigid rules with little explanation or flexibility. They prioritize obedience and control over emotional connection.

Children raised by authoritarian parents often:

- Lack self-esteem and confidence

- Struggle with social skills and forming healthy relationships

- Have difficulty regulating their emotions and can be prone to anxiety and depression

- May experience feelings of anger and resentment toward their parents

3. Permissive Parenting: This parenting style has high responsiveness and low demandingness. These parents are overly indulgent and lenient, rarely setting rules or enforcing expectations. They prioritize their children's happiness and avoid conflict at all costs.

Children raised by permissive parents may:

- Lack self-control and discipline

- Have difficulty regulating their emotions and managing frustration

- Struggle with academic achievement and responsibility

- May have difficulty forming healthy relationships due to unclear boundaries

4. Uninvolved Parenting: This revolves around low responsiveness and low demandingness. These parents are emotionally distant and uninvolved in their children's lives. They offer little to no guidance, support, or expectations.

Children raised by uninvolved parents often:

- Have low self-esteem and confidence

- Struggle with emotional regulation and social skills

- May experience feelings of neglect and insecurity

- Are more likely to engage in risky behaviors

These are broad categories, and individual parenting styles often fall somewhere on a spectrum between these extremes. Cultural context and personal experiences can also influence how these styles manifest and their impact on children. Baumrind's research remains one of the most influential in developmental psychology, but it's important to acknowledge that parenting is a complex and multifaceted process with numerous factors at play.

Overall, Baumrind's work highlights the crucial role of positive and supportive parenting styles in fostering healthy emotional adjustment and well-being in children. While no single style is perfect, parents who strive for a balance of responsiveness and demandingness are likely to create an environment that nurtures their children's emotional development and sets them up for success in life.

Build a home where expressions of love, empathy, and patience are woven into daily interactions.

Children raised in emotionally supportive environments are more likely to develop secure attachments, resilience, and a positive self-image. On the flip side, an emotionally tense or unpredictable climate may contribute to anxiety and behavioral challenges.

Social Interactions

The web of social interactions, both within the family and in broader social circles, becomes a dynamic influence on a child's social development.

A study by Sandra Simpkins and Douglas Downey, "Peer Group Formation and the Development of Social Capital in Early Childhood" (2010), examined the impact of early childhood friendships on children's social development. They found that having close and stable friendships in preschool was associated with:

Better social skills and emotional regulation: Children with strong friendships exhibited improved communication, conflict resolution, and empathy skills. They also demonstrated better ability to manage their emotions and cope with challenging situations.

Enhanced collaboration and teamwork: Children with strong friendships were more likely to work effectively with others, share resources, and participate in collaborative activities.

Greater understanding of social complexities: Through interactions with friends, children learn to confront social hierarchies, understand different perspectives, and adapt their behavior in various social situations.

The study emphasizes the importance of quality interactions over quantity. Meaningful friendships characterized by trust, communication, and mutual respect fostered the most significant developmental benefits. Early childhood settings like preschools and playgrounds can play a crucial role in facilitating these interactions and providing opportunities for children to develop their social skills.

The sandbox buzzed with activity. Ruby, clutching a plastic shovel, carefully sculpted a sandcastle, towers rising proudly. Suddenly, Pierce stomped in, kicking over a portion of her creation. Anger flared in Ruby's chest, but before she could unleash it, another voice interjected.

"Whoa, Pierce," said Teri, a kind-eyed girl with a playful grin. "Ruby worked hard on her castle. Maybe you can lend a hand instead?"

Pierce, momentarily taken aback, watched as Teri gently nudged a bucketful of sand toward the collapsed wall. Ruby, hesitation melting away, offered him a spare shovel. Soon, Pierce was giggling as he filled the gap, creating a taller, even more impressive tower.

This seemingly mundane interaction held deep significance. As Ruby and Pierce navigated their sandbox world, they were laying the groundwork for crucial social skills.

Positive interactions, like Teri's intervention, nurture important skills:

Sharing and cooperation: By working together, children learn the give-and-take of collaboration, fostering a sense of community and belonging.

Empathy and understanding: Observing others' emotions and responding with kindness, as Teri did, promotes the ability to see things from another's perspective.

Conflict resolution: Facing disagreements through communication and compromise, as Ruby and Pierce did, equips children with healthy tools for addressing future challenges.

Conversely, negative experiences can shape maladaptive behaviors:

Aggression and hostility: Witnessing or experiencing negativity can lead children to react similarly, hindering their ability to form healthy relationships.

Social isolation: Feeling excluded or ostracized can foster withdrawal and difficulty connecting with others.

Difficulty expressing emotions: Bottling up emotions or lacking healthy outlets for expression can lead to emotional dysregulation and social challenges.

The sandbox wasn't just a temporary play space; it was a microcosm of the social world Ruby and Pierce would experience throughout their lives. By fostering positive social environments where cooperation, empathy, and healthy conflict resolution are encouraged, we equip children with the skills they need to build strong, meaningful relationships and thrive in our complex social landscape.

Remember, every interaction, positive or negative, shapes a child's social development. Let's strive to create spaces where cooperation and kindness reign, building a future where everyone feels included and empowered to connect.

Educational Environment

For school-aged children, the educational environment becomes a crucial arena shaping their academic and intellectual growth. Educational psychology emphasizes that the classroom atmosphere, teaching methods, and peer interactions all contribute to a child's academic success and love for learning.

Robert Slavin, in his study, "Cooperative Learning in Elementary Mathematics: Do Small Groups Work?" (1990), found that students in cooperative learning groups showed significant gains in math achievement compared to those in individual settings. They also displayed improved problem-solving skills, critical thinking, and communication abilities. Importantly, students in cooperative groups reported higher levels of motivation and enjoyment toward learning math.

This study demonstrates the power of peer collaboration in fostering academic success and positive attitudes toward learning. By working together, students:

- Explain concepts to each other, solidifying their own understanding.

- Engage in active learning, participating more than in traditional lectures.

- Develop essential interpersonal skills like communication, collaboration, and conflict resolution.

- Experience a sense of community and belonging, boosting motivation and enjoyment.

This research aligns with educational psychology's emphasis on creating positive and engaging learning environments.

In the study "The Effect of Classroom Design on Student Engagement and Learning" (2015), it was observed how different classroom layouts and furniture arrangements impacted student behavior and attention span. It found that organized, clutter-free environments with fewer distractions improved student engagement and focus.

As a parent, you can work with your child's school to create a classroom where creativity is encouraged and diverse learning styles are embraced. This would foster a positive attitude toward learning and academic achievement. Conversely, a rigid or unsupportive educational setting may hinder a child's enthusiasm for education. This insight underscores the importance of advocating for educational environments that align with a child's individual strengths and needs.

Cultural and Societal Influences

The broader cultural and societal context in which a child grows up also exerts a profound influence on their beliefs, values, and identity formation. Cultural norms, traditions, and societal expectations shape a child's understanding of themselves and their place in the world.

Imagine a child exposed to diverse cultural experiences, fostering an appreciation for different perspectives. Such exposure contributes to cultural competence and open-mindedness. On the contrary, a narrow or prejudiced cultural environment may influence biased beliefs. This understanding emphasizes the role of cultural diversity in creating enriching environments that broaden a child's worldview.

Every Single Day Counts

In the warm glow of the kitchen, Jody watched her daughter, Elena, struggle with a button on her jacket. Frustration clouded Elena's face as tiny fingers fumbled, pulling and tugging in vain. Jody, remembering the sting of impatience she felt as a child under similar circumstances, knew the urge to intervene. But instead, she took a deep breath, channeling the wisdom gleaned from countless research studies on child development.

"Elena, sweetheart," she said gently, "how can I help you?"

Elena looked up, relief washing over her features. "Can you button it, Mommy?"

Jody smiled. "Of course I can, but I was wondering, could you try one more time? I know you can do it!"

Elena hesitated, then nodded, her determination returning. With newfound focus, she guided the button through the hole, a triumphant smile erupting as she finally secured it.

"See!" Jody exclaimed, her praise genuine, not just out of relief. "You did it all by yourself!"

This seemingly insignificant exchange served as an illustration of the complex act of parenting. It aligned with research findings such as those of Baumrind and Maccoby, emphasizing the critical role that parental support and responsiveness play in developing children's self-assurance and independence.

Jody knew patience wasn't just about waiting; it was about creating opportunities where the children could learn and grow. By resisting the urge to jump in, she allowed Elena to experience the satisfaction of overcoming a challenge, building her self-esteem and resilience.

Later that evening, Elena tackled a challenging math problem. Jody sat beside her, not providing answers but offering scaffolded support. She asked guiding questions, helping Elena break down the problem and reminding her of previously learned concepts. This approach mirrored research by Vygotsky, emphasizing the importance of the Zone of Proximal Development, where children learn best with just enough support to stretch their capabilities.

As Elena's brow furrowed in concentration, Jody offered encouragement, drawing inspiration from studies like Dweck's work on growth mindset. "Remember," she said, "Everyone makes mistakes, but that's how we learn and grow. You can do this!"

Finally, with a triumphant shout, Elena cracked the code. The joy in her eyes was a testament to the power of patience and support in nurturing a love for learning.

Jody knew that every interaction and every moment of patience shaped Elena's development. It wasn't always easy, but with research as her guide and love as her compass, she was shaping a future where Elena could confidently face any challenge, knowing she had the tools and the self-belief to succeed.

Now, let me guide you on how you can integrate such concepts into your own parenting life.

Modeling Behavior Each Day:

Research in developmental psychology emphasizes the profound impact of parental modeling on children's behavior. Bandura's Social Learning Theory underscores that children learn by observing the behaviors of those around them, particularly significant adults in their lives.

Bandura's theory suggests that children witnessing these behaviors are likely to internalize and replicate them in their own social interactions. This insight highlights the importance of mindful modeling, where our daily actions become a blueprint for the behaviors we hope to instill in our children.

The Patience Paradox:

Now, let's delve into the patience paradox. Research in child development, particularly the work of Diana Baumrind, a renowned clinical and developmental psychologist, sheds light on the significance of parental responsiveness and patience. Baumrind's studies identified authoritative parenting characterized by a balance of warmth, responsiveness, and reasonable expectations as conducive to optimal child outcomes.

Patiently guide your child through a challenging task rather than imposing strict demands. Baumrind's research suggests that authoritative parenting, with its emphasis on patience and responsiveness, fosters a secure attachment and promotes positive behavior in children. It's not about instant compliance but about nurturing a connection that lays the groundwork for emotional well-being.

Everyday Teachable Moments:

The concept of everyday teachable moments aligns with the socio-cultural theory of child development proposed by Lev Vygotsky. This theory posits that learning is a social process and occurs within the context of meaningful interactions. Everyday activities, conversations, and routines become opportunities for learning and skill development.

In Lya's kitchen, flour dusted the air like fallen snow. Her son, Lucas, perched on a stool and giggled as he stirred a gooey batter, his wooden spoon creating mesmerizing swirls. This wasn't just about making pancakes; it was a lesson in chemistry, physics, and even math, all unfolding within the comforting aroma of home.

The Vygotskian magic:

According to Lev Vygotsky's sociocultural theory, these everyday interactions create a "Zone of Proximal Development" (ZPD), a space where children, with adult guidance, can grasp concepts beyond their independent reach. Lya, acting as Lucas's "more knowledgeable other," frames his learning:

Breaking down complex tasks: Explaining how mixing ingredients creates a chemical reaction, how heat transforms batter into fluffy pancakes, and how fractions help measure the perfect sweetness.

Providing support: Guiding Lucas's hand as he cracks an egg, encouraging him to count as he adds sprinkles, and celebrating his "aha!" moments.

Fostering autonomy: Gradually handing over control, letting Lucas mix on his own, measure by himself, and eventually flip the pancakes with growing confidence.

The magic of Vygotskian learning extends far beyond the kitchen counter. From gardening to fixing a flat tire, everyday activities can become springboards for:

Science: Observing plant growth, understanding the forces behind a bicycle, or exploring the properties of water during bath time.

Math: Counting ingredients, measuring distances, or calculating recipe ratios—practical application brings math to life.

Language and communication: Explaining steps, asking questions, and discussing successes and challenges together.

Problem-solving: From figuring out how to make a smoother batter to troubleshooting a bike issue, children learn to think critically and find solutions.

Remember, it's not just about the activity itself; it's about infusing intentionality into these moments. Talk through the process, ask open-ended questions, celebrate discoveries, and encourage exploration.

By embracing Vygotskian learning, parents create countless benefits for their children:

Enhanced cognitive development: Improved problem-solving, critical thinking, and understanding of abstract concepts.

Stronger bonds and communication: Shared experiences deepen parent-child connections and create lasting memories.

Increased motivation and curiosity: Learning becomes an exciting adventure, fostering a love for exploration and knowledge.

Confidence and self-efficacy: Mastering new skills empowers children to tackle future challenges with independence and belief in themselves.

So, turn everyday moments into learning opportunities. Embrace the mess, the questions, and the wonder in your child's eyes. Remember, the kitchen, the garden, the driveway—they're not just spaces; they're potential classrooms waiting to unfold their magic. You, the ever-patient guide, are the key to unlocking a world of knowledge and empowering your child on their incredible journey of learning.

Long-Term Impact of Patience

Let's explore the long-term impact of parental patience through a lens informed by the Adverse Childhood Experiences (ACEs) study. The ACE study, conducted by the Centers for Disease Control and Prevention (CDC) and Kaiser Permanente, highlights the correlation between early adverse experiences and long-term health outcomes.

Imagine little Mily tripping and scraping her knee on the playground. Tears well up in her eyes, and she runs to her grandmother, seeking comfort. Instead of rushing to fix the scrape, Grandma kneels down, her voice calm and gentle. She patiently examines the wound, asks Mily how she's feeling, and explains what she's going to do to clean it. Lily feels heard and cared for, even though her knee stings.

This everyday scenario holds a deeper meaning based on the ACEs study, which explored the long-term effects of childhood adversity. It suggests that a patient and supportive environment can act like a shield, protecting children from the harmful impacts of negative experiences. Just like Grandma's calming presence eased Mily's pain, patience can build resilience and the inner strength to bounce back from challenges.

Here's how it works:

Think of resilience as a muscle: The more you exercise it, the stronger it gets. Patience and support from caregivers act like "resilience workouts."

Empathy and validation: When adults listen patiently and acknowledge children's feelings, even negative ones, they help them understand and process their emotions in a healthy way.

Positive communication: Words matter. Using calm, reassuring language instead of criticism or blame creates a safe space for children to express themselves and learn from their experiences.

Problem-solving together: Adults who patiently guide children through challenges, instead of fixing things for them, equip them with skills to navigate future difficulties confidently.

Celebrating small wins: Every step forward, no matter how small, deserves recognition. Patience allows adults to appreciate these victories, boosting children's self-esteem and motivation.

Just like Lily's scrape, not all adversities leave permanent scars. With the right support and a patient environment, children can develop the resilience to overcome challenges and thrive, even after difficult experiences.

Remember, patience isn't always easy, especially when children are emotional or struggling. But by taking a deep breath, staying calm, and offering understanding instead of quick fixes, you can create a protective shield of hardiness that will empower your child to face the world with confidence.

Strengthening Emotional Intelligence

Finally, let's touch upon the role of patience in cultivating emotional intelligence, drawing from the work of psychologists John Mayer, Peter Salovey, and Daniel Goleman. Emotional intelligence involves the ability to recognize, understand, and manage one's own emotions as well as those of others.

Imagine little Liam building a magnificent tower out of blocks, only to have it come crashing down with a loud clatter. Tears well up in his eyes, his face crumpling in frustration. This is a classic scenario where your approach can make a big difference in how Liam learns to handle his emotions.

Here's where Daniel Goleman's emotional intelligence framework comes in. It highlights five key areas that contribute to a child's emotional intelligence:

1. Self-awareness: Helping Liam recognize his emotions. You can say, "Oh dear, you look really upset. Is it because your tower fell down?" This helps him label his feelings and understand what's happening inside him.

2. Self-regulation: Guiding Liam to manage his emotions. Instead of rushing to rebuild the tower, sit with him and acknowledge his sadness. Offer calming breaths or a hug, suggesting, "Let's take a few deep breaths together and see how we can fix it." This teaches him healthy coping mechanisms.

3. Motivation: Encouraging Liam to persevere. Point out his previous successes, saying, "Remember how you rebuilt the tower even taller last time? We can do it again!" This fosters resilience and a positive attitude toward challenges.

4. Empathy: Showing Liam you understand his feelings. Validate his experience by saying, "I know it's frustrating when things fall apart, but we can try again!" This builds an emotional connection and shows him his feelings are acknowledged.

5. Social Skills: Helping Liam express his emotions constructively. Instead of bottling up his frustration, encourage him to communicate using words like "I'm feeling sad because the tower fell" or "I need help rebuilding it." This teaches him healthy communication skills during social situations.

By patiently guiding Liam through this emotional rollercoaster, you're not just rebuilding a tower; you're laying the foundation for his emotional intelligence. This will benefit him in various aspects of life:

At school: When facing academic challenges or disagreements with friends, he'll have the tools to manage his emotions and find solutions calmly.

In relationships: He'll be able to understand and respond to others' emotions, building stronger and healthier connections.

In his own well-being: He'll be better equipped to handle life's inevitable ups and downs with resilience and a positive outlook.

Remember, emotional intelligence is a journey, not a destination. By incorporating these principles into your daily interactions, you're equipping your child with valuable life skills that will empower them to navigate the world with confidence and emotional awareness.

Structuring Daily Routines

Imagine the whirlwind of family life: breakfast scrambles, school drop-offs, homework battles, and bedtime negotiations—a beautiful journey, yes, but one that can sometimes feel like a chaotic cacophony. Yet, amidst this orchestrated madness lies a powerful tool for bringing harmony: the daily routine.

Far from being rigid and restrictive, routines, like the conductor's baton, create the framework for a predictable and calming flow. They are not about stifling spontaneity; rather, they offer a foundation upon which flexibility can flourish.

Now, let's delve into it, exploring the significance of structured routines for both parents and children:

For Children

Predictability and security: Routines provide a sense of order and knowing what to expect, which can be immensely comforting for children. Imagine waking up every day to a familiar breakfast routine—it sets the tone for a calm and predictable day.

Development of life skills: Routines help children learn important skills like time management, responsibility, and independence. Packing their own backpack or setting the table for dinner fosters a sense of ownership and accomplishment.

Emotional regulation: Knowing what comes next can help children manage their emotions better. They are less likely to experience anxiety or meltdowns when they have a clear understanding of the daily flow.

Improved focus and learning: Consistent routines create a stable environment where children can focus on learning and activities. Think of it as preparing the stage for optimal performance.

For Parents

Reduced stress and chaos: Knowing what to expect and having a plan for the day can drastically reduce parental stress and anxiety. You can tackle tasks efficiently and avoid last-minute scrambling.

More quality time: Routines free up mental and emotional energy, allowing you to be more present and engaged with your children during quality time. It's like having the score memorized, allowing you to improvise and truly enjoy the music.

Stronger family bonds: Shared routines create a sense of unity and cooperation within the family. Working together to accomplish tasks fosters teamwork and strengthens the family bond.

Improved self-care: Routines can help you carve out time for self-care, whether it's exercise, meditation, or simply enjoying a quiet cup of coffee. Remember, a well-rested conductor leads to a more harmonious orchestra.

Let's remember that routines are not just about ticking off tasks; they are the melody that brings order, predictability, and countless benefits to the developmental landscape of our children and our own well-being. So, in the lovely chaos of family life, embrace the rhythm, hone the melody, and compose a symphony of harmony.

Creating a Sense of Security

Research in child development consistently underscores the importance of routines in providing a sense of security for children. The works of psychologists such as Mary Ainsworth, known for her research on attachment theory, highlight the role of predictable routines in establishing a secure base for exploration.

Lila's eyes fluttered open to the gentle melody of birdsong filtering through her window. A familiar warmth greeted her—the soft glow of her bedside lamp, a faint aroma of pancakes wafting from downstairs. A smile played on her lips, not only because it was Saturday but because this was just the beginning of her favorite routine.

Every morning, like clockwork, began the same way. Kevin, her father, tiptoed in, balancing a steaming mug of hot chocolate and a stack of fluffy pancakes precariously on a tray. Laughter and light conversation filled the room as they enjoyed their breakfast, followed by Lila helping Kevin make her favorite fruit salad. This wasn't just about pancakes and routine; it was about something much deeper, something Lila understood instinctively.

As Kevin tucked her back into bed after reading her a story, his voice hushed but warm, Lila felt a surge of security wash over her. This unwavering consistency, this predictable morning routine, resonated with the core of her being. It fueled her sense of trust, a trust that wasn't just in Kevin but in the world around her.

This understanding aligns with the work of Mary Ainsworth, a renowned psychologist who explored the impact of early relationships on child development. Her research, particularly the **Strange Situation Procedure**, highlighted the importance of secure attachment for healthy emotional development. Securely attached children, like Lila, have caregivers who are responsive, predictable, and reliable. This consistent, positive environment creates a sense of trust and security, empowering them to explore their surroundings with confidence and curiosity.

Lila's morning routine wasn't just a set of actions; it was a language of love and security. It communicated, "You are safe, you are loved, and you can trust the world around you." This strong foundation allowed Lila to blossom, embracing new experiences and challenges with the knowledge that her haven, her secure attachment, would always be there.

As Lila skipped downstairs, ready to face the day, she knew that whatever adventures awaited, her morning would play again tomorrow, reminding her that the world, despite its complexities, held a rhythm of love and reliability. And with that melody playing in her heart, she knew she could conquer anything.

Enhancing Emotional Regulation

Structured routines play a pivotal role in supporting children's emotional regulation. The work of child psychologist John Bowlby, a pioneer in attachment theory, suggests that consistent routines contribute to the development of self-regulation skills in children.

Picture a bedtime routine involving calming activities. Bowlby's insights indicate that this predictability helps children regulate their emotions, creating a soothing transition to sleep. The understanding here is that structured routines provide a framework for children to manage their emotional states, fostering resilience and coping skills.

As the sun dipped below the horizon, casting long shadows across Noah's room, a quiet magic unfolded. The day's activities began to slow, replaced by a gentler, more soothing rhythm. This was Noah's bedtime routine, a nightly ritual as comforting as a warm blanket on a chilly night.

John, Noah's father, entered the room, his voice soft and calming. Together, they embarked on their established journey:

Warm bath: The gentle lapping of water, scented with calming lavender oil, created a sensory haven. Noah giggled as John made playful, sudsy shapes, the playful interaction easing any lingering tension.

Storytime: John pulled out a well-worn book, its pages holding familiar tales that never failed to transport Noah to fantastical worlds. As John's voice wove through the narrative, Noah snuggled closer, his anxieties gradually melting away.

Calming music: As the bath ended, John switched on a playlist of soothing instrumental music. The soft melodies filled the room, replacing the day's noise with a sense of tranquility.

These seemingly simple activities resonate with the work of John Bowlby, a pioneer in attachment theory. Bowlby emphasized the importance of secure attachment in building healthy emotional development. He noted that consistent, predictable interactions create a safe space for children to develop trust and security.

Noah's bedtime routine mirrors these principles. It offers a predictable structure, a sheltered space where he knows what to expect and feels secure. This predictability, as Bowlby suggests, helps Noah regulate his emotions. The calming activities like storytelling, the warm bath, and the soothing music act as emotional anchors, guiding him away from anxieties and toward a state of relaxation.

The benefits of such routines extend beyond sleep. By providing a framework for managing emotions, bedtime routines equip children with valuable coping skills that benefit them throughout their lives. When faced with challenges or overwhelming emotions, they can draw upon the internalized calmness during their nightly rituals.

Think of it like building an emotional toolbox. Each calming activity adds a different tool—deep breathing exercises from mindful bath time, visualization techniques honed during story time, and self-soothing strategies learned through calming music. As children grow, these tools become readily available, empowering them through life's inevitable ups and downs with resilience and composure.

So, remember, bedtime routines are not just about getting children to sleep; they are about building emotional resilience, one calming activity at a time. As Noah drifted off to sleep, a peaceful smile on his face, John couldn't help but feel a sense of satisfaction. He was not just preparing his son for sleep; he was equipping him with the tools to face the world with confidence and emotional well-being.

Facilitating Skill Development

Daily routines serve as natural opportunities for skill development in children. The sociocultural theory of child development, as proposed by Lev Vygotsky in his study on "Mind in Society: The Development of Higher Psychological Processes," highlights the role of everyday activities in fostering cognitive and social skills.

Consider a routine where a child participates in setting the table for meals. Vygotsky's theory suggests that these structured activities contribute to the development of cognitive skills, social understanding, and a sense of responsibility. It's about leveraging routines as platforms for hands-on learning and skill acquisition within the context of daily life.

Creating Predictability for Parents

Structured routines aren't just beneficial for children; they also provide a sense of predictability and efficiency for parents. The Conservation of Resources theory, proposed by psychologist Stevan Hobfoll, suggests that individuals strive to conserve their resources, including time and energy, to maintain well-being.

Imagine a morning routine that allows parents to efficiently complete their tasks. Hobfoll's theory indicates that structured routines contribute to the conservation of parental resources, reducing stress and promoting overall well-being. This understanding emphasizes that well-organized routines benefit both children and parents by creating a more manageable daily flow.

You have now beautifully explored the multifaceted benefits of structured routines in family life. Just to wrap it up:

Imagine routines as the colors that enhance the canvas of family life. These colors, informed by research in child development, emotional regulation, and sleep, bind families together in a predictable, secure structure.

This allows children to flourish:

Emotionally: Routines build trust and security, promoting healthy emotional development.

Cognitively: Predictability allows children to focus on learning and exploring new skills.

Socially: Shared routines strengthen family bonds and boost cooperation.

And don't forget the benefits for parents:

Reduced stress: Knowing what to expect brings calm and organization.

More quality time: Predictable routines free up time for meaningful interactions.

Improved self-care: Consistent schedules allow parents to prioritize their well-being.

So, let's embrace the power of routines, not as rigid schedules but as flexible guidelines that create a harmonious rhythm for children and parents alike. Remember, the process of parenting needs both structure and space for improvisation to truly thrive.

Reducing Overstimulation

Imagine your child in a whirlwind, flashing lights, loud music, a constant barrage of new toys and activities. This, unfortunately, is a reality for many children in our fast-paced, technologically driven world. While enriching experiences are crucial for their development, the constant stimulation can be overwhelming, leading to what's known as overstimulation.

Moving on, we will draw upon insights from research in child psychology and practical parenting wisdom to help you:

• Recognize the signs of overstimulation in your child.

• Develop strategies to mitigate the overload and create a calmer environment.

• Find the sweet spot between enriching experiences and protecting your child from being overwhelmed.

Remember, the goal isn't to deprive your child of exciting experiences but to ensure they are delivered in a way that nurtures their development and promotes emotional well-being. Dive right in!

Understanding Overstimulation

Let's examine overstimulation from a psychological standpoint first to set the scene. A typical symptom of overstimulation in children is sensory overload, which happens when their sensory systems are overstimulated beyond their capacity to handle it. According to psychologist Elaine Aron's research on sensory processing sensitivity, certain people—including kids—are more vulnerable to being overstimulated.

Envision a busy play area filled with lots of activities, bright lights, and loud noises. According to Aron's observations, a setting like this could easily result in overstimulation in kids who are sensitive to sensory information. This knowledge highlights how crucial it is to acknowledge individual differences and modify surroundings to meet the needs of every child.

Creating Calm Spaces

Incorporating calm spaces within our homes becomes a practical strategy for reducing overstimulation. Research in environmental psychology, as demonstrated by studies like those by Roger S. Ulrich, suggests that exposure to natural elements and serene environments can have a positive impact on stress reduction and well-being.

Imagine walking into a playroom bursting with energy—colorful toys piled high, flashing lights from electronic games, and excited children zipping around. While this might seem like a dream play space for some, for others, particularly children with Sensory Processing Sensitivity (SPS), as identified by Elaine Aron, it could be a recipe for overload.

Understanding SPS:

Aron's research suggests that some individuals are born with a heightened sensitivity to sensory stimuli like sights, sounds, smells, and textures. This means they process information from their environment more intensely, which can be both a blessing and a curse. While it can lead to a deeper appreciation for beauty and detail, it can also easily result in overstimulation in overwhelming environments.

Overstimulation in action:

Back to our busy playroom. For a child with SPS, the flashing lights might feel like strobe lights, the loud noises like sonic booms, and the abundance of toys a confusing jumble. This bombardment of sensory information can trigger various reactions, including:

Irritability and meltdowns: Feeling overwhelmed can lead to frustration, crying, or even aggressive behavior.

Difficulties focusing and regulating emotions: The child might struggle to concentrate amidst the chaos, leading to emotional dysregulation.

Withdrawal and avoidance: Seeking solace in quieter spaces to escape the overwhelming stimuli.

Tailoring the environment:

Recognizing these signs and understanding individual differences is crucial. While we can't control every environment, there are ways to adapt our approach to support children with SPS:

Offer quieter alternatives: Provide a designated calm corner with calming toys and soft lighting.

Limit exposure to intense stimuli: Rotate toys regularly, dim lights when possible, and offer noise-canceling headphones.

Prepare for transitions: Warn children about upcoming changes in stimulation, like leaving a quiet space for a noisy playground.

Embrace individual preferences: Observe what specific stimuli bother your child and adjust accordingly.

Remember, every child is unique, and what works for one might not work for another. The key is to be mindful, observe their reactions, and create a nurturing environment that allows them to explore and thrive without feeling overwhelmed. By doing so, we can ensure that the "playroom of life" becomes a space of joy, discovery, and well-being for all children.

Balancing Screen Time

In today's technological age, controlling screen time is essential to lowering overstimulation. Studies, like those conducted by Jean M. Twenge, demonstrate the possible negative effects of prolonged screen time on kids' health, including an increased chance of behavioral problems and sleep difficulties.

Consider a deliberate strategy for screen usage, with specific times set aside for using technology. According to Twenge's study, these well-rounded strategies support more positive developmental outcomes. This realization emphasizes how crucial it is to establish boundaries and encourage activities that provide our kids with a more balanced sensory environment.

Promoting Mindful Play

Mindful play becomes a valuable tool in reducing overstimulation. Research in developmental psychology, drawing from the works of Jean Piaget, suggests that play serves as a crucial avenue for children to explore and make sense of their world.

Imagine a child giggling as they build a towering castle, their imagination soaring with each block placed. This scenario embodies the ideal we strive for—play environments that nurture both exploration and emotional well-being. Drawing on insights from Piaget's theory of cognitive development, we can create spaces that minimize overstimulation while maximizing learning and fun.

Piaget's perspective:

Piaget identified different stages of cognitive development in children, where their play reflects their understanding of the world. By matching play activities to their developmental stage, we can engage them without overwhelming them.

Here are some ideas categorized by age group:

Toddlers (1-3 years old):

Open-ended toys: Blocks, buckets, stacking cups, and play dough encourage creativity and exploration.

Sensory experiences: Water play, sandboxes, and textured toys engage their senses and curiosity.

Simple musical instruments: Drums, shakers, and rhythm sticks allow exploration of sound and movement.

Limit screens: Excessive screen time can be overstimulating for this age group.

Preschoolers (3-5 years old):

Dress-up clothes and props: Spark imaginative play and role-playing.

Arts and crafts: Painting, drawing, and clay molding help develop fine motor skills and expression.

Construction sets: Legos, Magna Tiles, and wooden blocks encourage problem-solving and spatial reasoning.

Cooperative games: Puzzles, board games, and simple sports foster social interaction and turn-taking skills.

Limit screen time: Continue to monitor screen time and choose educational content when applicable.

School-aged Children (6-10 years old)

Creative kits: Science experiments, art kits, and building sets offer engaging challenges.

Group games: Board games, card games, and sports promote social interaction and strategic thinking.

Musical instruments: Learning an instrument fosters creativity and discipline.

Reading nooks: Provide comfortable spaces for quiet reading and imagination.

Manage screen time: Set clear rules and encourage alternative activities.

Beyond Specific Toys

Create designated play areas: This helps children organize their thoughts and activities.

Rotate toys regularly: Keeps things fresh and prevents overstimulation.

Engage in play with your child: This shows them the value of play and creates lasting memories.

Offer choices: Allowing children to choose their play activities fosters autonomy and engagement.

Observe and adjust: Pay attention to their reactions and modify the environment if needed.

Be mindful of your child's individual needs and preferences. By creating a play environment that encourages exploration without overwhelming them, you're encouraging not just fun but cognitive and emotional development, setting them up for a lifetime of joyful learning.

Establishing Predictable Routines

Structured routines, as discussed earlier, play a dual role in reducing overstimulation. Research in child development, including studies by Celeste Kidd, suggests that predictable routines provide a sense of order and familiarity, reducing cognitive load and stress.

Imagine a daily routine that integrates consistent meal times and sleep schedules. Kidd's research implies that such routines contribute to a more predictable environment, helping children pass their day with less cognitive strain. This insight underscores the importance of maintaining a balance between novelty and predictability in daily activities.

Encouraging Mindful Parenting

Lastly, the concept of mindful parenting becomes a crucial element in reducing overstimulation. Research by Susan L. Smalley indicates that mindfulness practices, such as meditation and mindful awareness, can positively impact parent-child interactions and contribute to overall family well-being.

The sun peeked through the curtains, bathing Amelia's room in a warm glow. Amelia, however, squeezed her eyes shut, the morning light feeling jarring. Sandy, Amelia's mother, noticed this immediately. Taking a deep breath, she remembered the tips from her parenting group about Smalley's mindfulness research.

Instead of rushing in with bright greetings, Sandy gently whispered, "Good morning, sleepyhead. Would you like me to open the curtains slowly?"

Amelia nodded, a tiny smile peeking through her eyelashes. Sandy responded with a warm smile of her own, opening the curtains bit by bit, allowing the light to gently adjust to Amelia's sensitive eyes. This small, mindful act set the tone for the day.

Throughout the morning, Sandy remained present and attuned to Amelia's cues. When Amelia seemed overwhelmed by the noise of the bustling kitchen, Sandy offered her a pair of noise-canceling headphones and a quiet corner with building blocks. During story time, she noticed Amelia fidgeting, so she suggested a few mindful stretches and deep breaths, calming their bodies and minds together.

As the day unfolded, Sandy didn't forget the bigger picture. She limited screen time, opting for outdoor adventures and creative play with open-ended toys. Predictable routines offered a sense of comfort and security, reducing unexpected stressors. Bedtime was a haven of calming music and snuggles, easing Amelia into a peaceful sleep.

Reflecting on the day, Sandy felt a sense of satisfaction. By incorporating mindfulness into her parenting, she not only minimized instances of overstimulation but also built a stronger connection with her daughter. She understood that creating a nurturing environment wasn't just about external factors; it began with her own inner calmness and awareness.

Remember, dear reader, by recognizing individual needs, creating calming spaces, and making mindful choices, we can cultivate environments that nurture, soothe, and allow our children to blossom, one present moment at a time.

Chapter 5: Building Emotional Intelligence

Think about the last time your little one had a meltdown because their sandwich was cut into squares instead of triangles. Frustrating, right? Or how about when your teen rolled their eyes so hard you thought they'd get stuck that way? Parenting is undeniably an emotional rollercoaster, and sometimes it feels like you need superpowers to get through the day. That's where Emotional Intelligence (EI) swoops in.

So, what is emotional intelligence? Imagine it as your secret toolkit for understanding and managing emotions. It's about being the cool-headed detective who figures out what's behind those tantrums or moods rather than the sheriff who's ready to lay down the law without a clue.

Emotional intelligence starts with awareness. It is like turning on an emotional GPS to navigate your child's feelings and your own. It's knowing that when your kid is kicking and screaming, they might not just be acting up—they could be tired, overwhelmed, or just hungry for that oddly specific triangle-shaped sandwich.

The next step is all about connection. Once you tune into those feelings, empathy becomes your best friend. It's like putting yourself in their tiny shoes and understanding the world from their pint-sized perspective.

Then comes the part where we teach by practicing what we preach. If you tackle your own frustration by counting to ten or taking deep breaths, you'll be amazed when your kids start doing the same.

Communication is the cherry on top. It's choosing a calm chat over a shouting match, using words that aren't drenched in emotion. It's about setting the stage for open, honest talks because when they are dealing with bigger life stuff than sandwich shapes, you will want them to come to you.

Being a parent with high emotional intelligence doesn't mean you have all the answers or are always cool as a cucumber. It's about being honest, present, and understanding that you and your child are on a learning journey—together.

Remember, it is a marathon, not a sprint. So lace up those emotional sneakers and get ready for one of the most rewarding runs of your life—raising kids with a whole lot of heart, smarts, and the emotional muscle to tackle whatever comes their way.

Emotional intelligence, as interpreted by psychologists Peter Salovey and John D. Mayer, comprises four fundamental components:

1. Perceiving Emotions: The ability to accurately recognize and interpret emotions in oneself and others.

2. Using Emotions: Harnessing emotions to facilitate cognitive processes and decision-making.

3. Understanding Emotions: Grasping the nuances and complexities of emotions, discerning their causes and effects.

4. Managing Emotions: Taking control of one's own emotions and effectively handling interpersonal dynamics.

Let me help you understand through the following story.

Luna was happily bouncing a tennis ball off the living room wall. Each thwack resonated with her mother Kelly's growing headache.

"Luna, sweetheart," she began, trying to keep her voice patient. "Remember what we talked about?"

Luna paused, mid-bounce, a defiant scowl twisting her features.

"No fun," she mumbled, kicking the ball across the room.

Kelly recognized the frustration bubbling beneath Luna's defiance (perceiving emotions). This wasn't just about the ball but about wanting to play outside despite the rain (understanding emotions). Taking a deep breath, Kelly used her own frustration as a motivator (using emotions) to find a solution.

"I know, honey," she knelt and met Luna's gaze.

"The rain is a bummer, but let's brainstorm some fun indoor activities. How about building a blanket fort and having a picnic lunch inside?"

Luna's scowl softened. Building forts was always an adventure. "Can we have pizza in the fort?" she asked, her eyes sparkling.

"Absolutely!" Kelly smiled, relieved. She'd managed her own emotions (managing emotions) and redirected Luna's negative energy into a positive solution.

Building the fort became an exercise in teamwork and creativity. Kelly praised Luna's ideas, encouraging her confidence and emotional expression. Their laughter echoed through the living room, replacing the earlier tension.

Later, snuggled inside the fort, munching on pizza, Luna confided, "I was feeling sad because I couldn't play outside."

Kelly, heartened by Luna's openness, responded, "It's okay to feel sad, honey. Sometimes, bad weather throws even the best plans off course. But we can still have fun like this!"

At that moment, Kelly wasn't just Luna's mom; she was a teammate, a confidante, and an emotional guide. By employing the four pillars of emotional intelligence (perceiving, using, understanding, managing), she transformed a potentially explosive situation into a positive bonding experience. Luna, in turn, learned to express her emotions healthily and overthrow challenges constructively.

As the evening wore on, Kelly realized that emotional intelligence wasn't just a psychological theory; it was the magic ingredient that turned ordinary moments into extraordinary connections, shaping not just a fun night but a deeper, more emotionally attuned mother-daughter bond.

I sincerely hope that you understood the message as well as Kelly did. Here are some tips regarding the steps you can follow to incorporate them into your daily life.

1. Be a perceptive mirror

Observe your child's emotions: Notice their facial expressions, body language, and tone of voice. Pay attention to changes in their behavior.

Validate their feelings: Don't dismiss their emotions as "silly" or "wrong." Acknowledge their feelings with phrases like, "I see you're feeling frustrated" or "It sounds like you're disappointed."

2. Use emotions as a guide

Understand the cause: What triggered their emotion? Are they tired, hungry, overwhelmed?

Observe body language and facial expressions: Pay attention to nonverbal cues to understand how others might be feeling. Try putting yourself in their shoes.

Ask open-ended questions: Encourage communication by prompting your child to express their thoughts and feelings.

Offer alternatives: Instead of saying "no," suggest other ways to fulfill their needs. Offer choices like, "Would you like to read a book or build with blocks instead?"

3. Deepen your emotional understanding

Learn about child development: Each age has its own emotional challenges. Understanding these can help you anticipate and deal with them.

Reflect on your own emotions: How are you feeling in the moment? Are your own emotions influencing your response?

Harness positive emotions: Channel excitement and motivation into productive action.

Transform negative emotions: Use frustration as a catalyst for finding solutions and sadness as an opportunity for self-compassion.

4. Manage your own emotions

Take a breath: Before reacting, take a moment to calm yourself down. Identify what you're feeling. Are you frustrated, anxious, or overwhelmed? This will help you analyze yourself and respond thoughtfully, not impulsively.

Use journaling or mindfulness exercises: Regularly reflect on your emotions and patterns to better understand yourself. Exercise, meditation, or spending time in nature can help regulate your emotions.

Practice self-care: Make time for activities that help you manage stress and stay emotionally regulated.

5. Foster a supportive environment

Encourage open communication: Create a safe space where your child feels comfortable expressing their emotions, even negative ones. Express your needs and feelings clearly and respectfully while considering the other person's perspective.

Celebrate emotional expression: Praise your child for identifying and expressing their emotions in healthy ways. Don't expect immediate results. Celebrate small wins and learn from setbacks.

Be a role model: Show your child how to manage your own emotions in healthy ways.

By applying these steps, you can channel your emotions to channel in the right way effectively, just like Kelly guided Luna. Remember, emotional intelligence is a skill that grows with practice. So, embark on your journey with self-compassion and a belief in your ability to change and thrive!

Why is Emotional Intelligence Important?

Imagine parenting with x-ray vision, seeing not just your child's actions but the feelings behind them. That's the power of Emotional Intelligence (EQ). According to a 2021 study in Developmental Psychology, kids with high EQ have better social skills, understand others' feelings easier, and cope with challenges calmly.

Why is emotional intelligence not just a skill but a fundamental necessity in life? The answer lies in its profound impact on personal well-being, relationships, and overall success. Let's peel off the layers one by one and understand why fostering emotional intelligence is akin to providing our children with a compass that boosts their overall life experience.

1. Enhancing Interpersonal Relationships:

At the heart of emotional intelligence lies the ability to understand and manage the emotions of oneself and others. This proficiency becomes the bedrock of meaningful relationships. Children equipped with emotional intelligence are adept at recognizing and responding to the feelings of their peers, family members, and friends. This heightened sensitivity cultivates empathy, forging connections that are built on mutual understanding and support.

Goleman, D. (2006) stated that children with a high EQ (Emotional Quotient) understand and respond to others' feelings, leading to stronger social bonds. They are also better able to put themselves in others' shoes, fostering compassion and understanding, according to Eisenberg, N., & Fabes, R. A. (2008).

2. Effective Communication:

Communication transcends mere words; it's a combination of emotions and unspoken cues. Emotional intelligence empowers children with the skill to articulate their feelings, needs, and thoughts effectively. Whether expressing joy, frustration, or concern, children with well-developed emotional intelligence can communicate with clarity, fostering open and constructive dialogues in various aspects of their lives.

3. Tackling Life's Challenges:

Life is a rollercoaster of emotions, and resilience in the face of challenges is one of the key characteristics of high emotional intelligence. Children equipped with this skill are better prepared to confront setbacks, manage stress, and adapt to changing circumstances. They develop a robust internal system that guides them through the highs and lows, enabling them to bounce back from adversity with grace and determination.

4. Building Self-Awareness:

Understanding oneself is the foundation of personal growth. Emotional intelligence provides children with directions to control their own emotions, motivations, and reactions. This self-awareness becomes vital for making informed decisions, setting realistic goals, and nurturing a positive self-image. It lays the groundwork for a strong sense of identity and purpose.

5. Academic Success:

Emotional intelligence extends its influence into the academic realm. Children with high emotional intelligence often exhibit better problem-solving skills, higher levels of motivation, and improved academic performance. The ability to manage stress and form positive relationships with teachers and peers contributes to a conducive learning environment.

Research from the University of California, Berkeley, has also suggested that higher EQ in childhood leads to greater academic success and career satisfaction in adulthood.

6. Conflict Resolution:

Conflicts are inevitable in life, but how we tackle them defines the quality of our relationships. Emotional intelligence equips children with the skills to manage conflicts constructively. By understanding their own emotions and empathizing with others, they can find common ground, negotiate effectively, and resolve disputes without escalating tensions.

7. Empowering Decision-Making:

Life is a series of decisions, and emotional intelligence serves as a guiding force in the decision-making process. Children with this skill assess situations with emotional acuity, weigh the potential outcomes, and make decisions aligned with their values and long-term goals. This ability contributes to a sense of agency and autonomy.

8. Fostering Mental Health:

Emotional intelligence acts as a shield against the negative impacts of stress and emotional turmoil. Children who can manage their emotions effectively are less prone to anxiety and depression. The ability to express, understand, and control emotions promotes mental well-being and resilience, laying the groundwork for a healthier and more fulfilling life.

Well, you must surely be wishing to develop this superpower and make your child the living proof of these findings. Wait no more because I have just the right solution!

Think of yourself as their emotional trainer. Here are some key moves:

Be their mirror: Help them name their feelings. When your child throws a tantrum, instead of saying, "Stop crying!" say, "I see you're frustrated. Is something bothering you?" This validates their emotions and opens the door for communication.

Play detective: Notice their reactions. Did they frown at that comment? Does their face light up when they're praised? Talk about these non-verbal cues, like "I noticed you seemed shy when talking to that new friend," to build their self-awareness.

Be their coach: Don't just solve problems, guide the kids through them. When they have a conflict, ask questions like "How do you think your friend might be feeling?" and "What could you do differently next time?" This equips them with problem-solving skills.

Practice makes perfect: Model healthy ways to handle emotions. Feeling stressed? Take deep breaths and talk about it calmly. Dealing with anger? Take a break and come back to the conversation later. Your child learns by watching you.

Remember, parenting is a journey. Be patient, celebrate small wins, and enjoy the process of watching your child blossom!

Tackling Tantrums

The sight of a child in the throes of a tantrum can trigger anxiety and frustration in even the calmest parent. Screams pierce the air, limbs flail, and tears paint a picture of utter distress. While these outbursts can test our patience, research suggests that tantrums, although challenging, are actually windows into a child's developing emotional world.

Studies by Cole et al. (2002) and Thompson et al. (1998) show that tantrums often emerge due to limited emotional regulation skills and frustration at communicating needs. Just like adults, children experience a range of emotions—anger, sadness, fear—but lack the vocabulary and cognitive tools to express them effectively.

This is where the concept of Emotional Intelligence (EQ) enters the picture. Defined as the ability to understand, use, and manage emotions effectively, EQ has been linked to increased resilience, empathy, and social competence in children (Denham et al., 2003).

In the context of tantrums, adopting EQ in parents plays a crucial role. Studies by Gottman & Gottman (1997) and Eisenberg et al. (2006) demonstrate that parents who respond with empathy, understanding, and emotional regulation techniques can not only de-escalate tantrums but also teach their children valuable emotional coping skills.

So, while tantrums may seem like temporary storms, embracing emotional intelligence can transform them into opportunities for growth and connection.

Join me on a journey beyond frustration and discover the transformative power of an emotionally intelligent approach to parenting.

The supermarket checkout buzzed with a relentless hum, a backdrop to Penny's growing dread. Two-year-old Kale, usually a ball of sunshine, lay sprawled on the floor, arms flailing, emitting a banshee wail that could shatter glass.

"No cereal!" he shrieked, snot mixing with tears as he kicked a discarded magazine.

Penny felt her face flush. Shame and frustration battled within her. Why did this always happen in public? Judging eyes seemed to bore into her back, whispering accusations of bad parenting. Taking a deep breath, she knelt beside Kale, ignoring the urge to yank him up.

"Kale, I hear you're upset," she said calmly, using the "I" statement she'd learned in a parenting class.

"We talked about getting oatmeal this morning, remember?"

Kale's wails intensified. "Cereal! Me want cereal!"

Instead of arguing, Penny validated his feelings. "I know you wanted cereal, honey. But we can't get it today. How about we choose a fun fruit for your oatmeal?"

Silence. Kale's tear flow subsided, replaced by a sniffle. He peeked up at her, suspicion lingering in his eyes. Penny smiled encouragingly, offering him a choice between strawberries and blueberries.

Hesitantly, Kale pointed to the blueberries. Penny praised his choice, her heart sinking with relief. They passed through the remaining checkout line, with Kale munching happily on his berries and the tantrum seemingly a distant memory.

The tantrum had been rough, but by using emotional intelligence, acknowledging his feelings, offering choices, and staying calm, Penny had tackled it without resorting to yelling or giving in. It wasn't always easy, but these small victories fueled her hope. Each tantrum conquered, each emotion validated, strengthened their bond, and taught Kale valuable lessons about managing his emotions.

Understanding the Roots of Tantrums

Before we delve into strategies for correction, it's crucial to grasp the roots of tantrums. Tantrums often stem from a child's inability to effectively communicate their emotions or fulfill a need. It's a cry for understanding, attention, or autonomy. Recognizing this foundation sets the stage for an empathetic and constructive approach to correction.

1. Stay Calm and Centered:

In the face of a tantrum, it's easy to be swept up in the emotional whirlwind. However, emotional intelligence begins with the ability to regulate our own emotions. By staying calm and centered, parents model the emotional resilience they hope to instill in their children. Take a deep breath, center yourself, and approach the situation with a composed demeanor.

2. Validate Emotions:

Emotional intelligence involves recognizing and validating emotions, even when they manifest in challenging ways. Begin by acknowledging your child's feelings. Phrases like "I see that you're upset" or "It looks like you're feeling frustrated" communicate empathy and understanding. This acknowledgment doesn't mean condoning the behavior but rather validating the underlying emotions.

3. Provide Verbal Expression:

Encourage your child to express their feelings verbally. For younger children who may struggle with articulation, offer simple phrases they can repeat, like "I'm mad" or "I need help." Verbal expression helps them transition from emotional outbursts to a more constructive form of communication.

4. Offer Choices:

Empower your child with a sense of autonomy by providing choices. For instance, if the tantrum revolves around a specific task, offer alternatives. This not only redirects their focus but also allows them to feel a sense of control, fostering emotional intelligence by promoting decision-making skills.

5. Teach Emotional Regulation Techniques:

As emotions run high, it's essential to equip your child with tools for emotional regulation. Simple techniques like deep breathing or counting to ten can be introduced during calm moments, so they become familiar strategies during moments of distress. This lays the foundation for self-regulation, a key component of emotional intelligence.

6. Establish Clear Boundaries:

While understanding and empathy are crucial, it's equally important to set clear boundaries. Communicate acceptable behavior and the consequences of crossing those boundaries. Consistency in enforcing these boundaries provides a structured framework within which emotional intelligence can flourish.

7. Reinforce Positive Behavior:

Positive reinforcement is a powerful tool in shaping behavior. When your child successfully navigates a challenging moment or expresses their emotions more constructively, acknowledge and praise their efforts. This positive reinforcement reinforces the connection between emotional intelligence and positive outcomes.

8. Adopt Problem-Solving Skills:

Tantrums often arise from frustration when children encounter obstacles. Encourage problem-solving by involving your child in finding solutions. This not only promotes critical thinking but also enhances their ability to face challenges with a more composed and solution-oriented approach.

9. Reflect and Debrief:

After the storm subsides, take a moment to reflect and debrief with your child. Ask them about their feelings, what triggered the tantrum, and how they could handle a similar situation differently in the future. This reflective process promotes self-awareness and learning from emotional experiences.

10. Seek Professional Guidance if Needed:

If tantrums persist or escalate to concerning levels, seeking guidance from a child psychologist or behavioral specialist can provide additional insights and strategies tailored to your child's unique needs.

Identifying Emotions

Picture this: Your child comes home from school, throws their backpack down with a thud, and storms off to their room. Frustration bubbles inside you, but before you launch into a lecture, take a deep breath. Turns out, there's a better way to navigate this emotional rollercoaster, one paved with Emotional Intelligence (EQ)!

Here's the science behind the magic: studies by Saarni (1999) and Dunn et al. (2002) show that children who can identify and name their emotions experience a cascade of benefits. They develop better self-awareness, communicate more effectively, and even cope with challenges more resiliently. So, how do we help them unlock this superpower?

Let's ditch the "big boy/big girl" talk and dive into some fun strategies:

1. Mirror, Mirror on the Wall: When your child throws a tantrum or expresses strong emotions, reflect them back in a calm and validating way. For example, instead of saying, "Don't be silly," try, "I see you're feeling frustrated. Can you tell me what happened?" This helps them label their emotions and feel understood.

2. Emoji Adventure: Emotions can be tricky, especially for little ones. Use emojis, pictures, or even color charts to create a visual dictionary of emotions. When your child feels overwhelmed, they can point to the chart and say, "I feel like the red angry face!" This helps them build their emotional vocabulary and express themselves more clearly.

3. Story Time with Emotions: Turn bedtime stories into emotional learning experiences. Pause at key moments and ask your child, "How do you think the character is feeling right now?" Discuss different emotions and their causes. This helps them connect emotions to situations and develop empathy.

4. The Feelings Game: Make learning fun! Play charades with emotions, draw pictures representing different moods, or even create a "feelings jar" where everyone can write down their emotions on slips of paper. This playful approach makes identifying emotions less daunting and more engaging.

Some ideas to help enhance your parenting with a touch of EQ!

1. Create an Emotionally Rich Environment: Begin by cultivating an environment that highlights diverse emotions. Picture books with expressive characters, interactive games that explore feelings, and casual conversations that include emotional vocabulary create an emotionally rich landscape for children to navigate.

2. Emotion Charades: Transforming the learning process into a playful activity that engages in emotion charades. Encourage your child to express emotions through facial expressions and body language while others guess the emotion. This interactive game not only makes learning fun but also enhances their ability to recognize and embody different feelings.

3. The Emotion Mirror: Set up an "emotion mirror" activity where your child mimics different facial expressions you make. Label each expression with the corresponding emotion, creating a visual and kinesthetic connection between facial cues and feelings. This activity not only reinforces emotional recognition but also strengthens the empathy component of Emotional Intelligence.

4. Emotion Journal: Introduce the concept of an emotion journal where your child can doodle or write about their feelings. Encourage them to express what made them feel a certain way and explore the nuances of each emotion. This reflective practice fosters self-awareness and provides a tangible record of their emotional journey.

5. Storytelling with Emotions: Utilize storytelling as a powerful tool to explore emotions. Choose stories that vividly depict characters experiencing a range of feelings. Pause during the narrative to discuss the emotions characters are experiencing and ask your child to share instances when they felt similar emotions. This interactive storytelling nurtures emotional literacy.

6. Emotion Cards: Create or use emotion cards featuring different facial expressions. Shuffle the cards and ask your child to match each expression with the corresponding emotion. This tactile and visual activity reinforces the association between facial cues and emotions, enhancing their recognition skills.

7. Emotion Walk: Take a stroll together and turn it into an "emotion walk." During the walk, ask your child to identify and name the emotions they observe in others, whether it's people passing by, neighbors, or even animals. This real-world application enhances their ability to recognize emotions in diverse contexts.

8. Personalized Feelings Chart: Collaboratively create a personalized feelings chart with your child. Use colorful markers, pictures, or stickers to represent different emotions. Hang the chart in a visible place, and regularly discuss and update it based on your child's evolving emotional experiences.

9. Empathy Role Play: Engage in role-playing scenarios that evoke specific emotions. Take turns playing different characters and explore how each one feels in various situations. This experiential activity not only enhances emotional recognition but also nurtures empathy as children step into the shoes of others.

10. Open Emotional Dialogues: Encourage open and non-judgmental dialogues about emotions. Create a safe space for your child to express their feelings without fear of criticism. When they share an emotion, ask open-ended questions to delve deeper into their experience and help them articulate the nuances of what they're feeling.

Remember, patience is key. It takes time and practice for children to master the art of identifying their emotions. Celebrate their efforts, offer gentle guidance, and, most importantly, have fun along the way! So, go forth and decode those dragons together—one emotion-filled adventure at a time!

Story time!

Daniel slammed the comic book down on the table, sending a tremor through the breakfast dishes. His father, Sean, a man usually calm as a summer breeze, couldn't ignore the tempest brewing in his son's eyes.

"Rough morning, buddy?" Sean asked, his voice gentle.

"Worst ever," Daniel mumbled, pushing his cereal around the bowl like an angry gladiator.

Sean knew there was more to it than just a bad breakfast. He remembered a similar storm brewing a few weeks ago when Daniel's soccer team lost a game. But back then, Sean had tried the usual "toughen up" approach, and it hadn't worked. This time, he decided to try something different.

"Remember what we talked about last week? About emotions being like colors?"

Daniel, ever the inquisitive seven-year-old, looked up, a flicker of interest sparking in his eyes.

"Yeah," he mumbled, the anger momentarily forgotten.

Sean smiled. "Okay, so what color do you feel inside you right now?"

Daniel thought for a moment, scrunching his nose. "Red, like angry fire red."

"And why is it fire red?" Sean encouraged, taking a sip of his coffee.

"Because Mrs. Henderson wouldn't let me bring my dinosaur toy to show-and-tell," Daniel explained, his voice rising again. "It's the coolest dinosaur ever, and everyone would've loved it!"

Sean saw the injustice burning in his son's eyes, the disappointment at not being able to share his passion. He nodded, understanding.

"It's okay to be angry, Daniel," Sean said calmly. "But sometimes, fire red can lead to meltdowns, just like a volcano erupting. What other colors can we use to express how you feel?"

Daniel pondered, chewing his lip. "Maybe... orange, like the setting sun? Because I'm sad too, that I couldn't show everyone my dino."

Sean's heart warmed. "Exactly! And maybe a little blue, like the ocean, because you feel left out?"

Daniel's eyes widened. "Yeah! And maybe even a tiny bit of green because I'm jealous of the other kids who got to bring their toys."

Sean chuckled. "See, there are so many colors to your emotions, not just fire red. And each color tells a story."

Over the next few weeks, Daniel and Sean continued their exploration of the emotional color palette. They identified yellow for happiness, purple for frustration, and even black for fear. Each night, they'd share their emotional landscapes, painting vivid pictures with words.

Slowly, Daniel's tantrums became less frequent, replaced by open communication and a deeper understanding of his own feelings. He learned to express himself clearly, using his "emotional color chart" to navigate the complexities of his inner world.

And Sean? He discovered the immense power of emotional intelligence in parenting. By truly listening and validating his son's feelings, he had built a bridge of understanding, transforming tantrums into opportunities for connection and growth. In the end, their journey with emotions wasn't just about managing Daniel's outbursts; it was about painting a masterpiece of father-son understanding, one colorful brushstroke at a time.

Empowering with Coping Strategies

Picture this: your kid is having a meltdown, tears streaming down their face like a mini waterfall. You're tempted to yell, bribe, or maybe just hide under the couch. But hold on, superhero parent! I am pleased to tell you that there's a better way. Enter coping strategies, the secret weapons in your emotional intelligence arsenal.

Think of it like this: Emotions are like waves. Sometimes, they're gentle ripples, other times, they're crashing breakers. Coping strategies are like surfboards, helping your child ride those waves without getting wiped out.

Here's the cool part: Studies by folks like Dunsmore & Ollendick (2014) and Leparent et al. (2000) show that teaching kids coping strategies early on can make a big difference. Not only does it help them handle tough emotions at the moment, but it also builds resilience for the future, making them better equipped to deal with whatever life throws their way.

So, get ready to equip yourself with the perfect weapons that you need along the way. We'll explore things like deep breathing exercises, mindfulness techniques, and even creative expression. Remember, there's no one-size-fits-all approach, so we'll equip you with the tools to tailor these strategies to your child's unique personality and needs.

Get ready to witness the power of emotional intelligence in action! Let's help your child walk their emotional landscape with confidence and grace, turning those tantrums into triumphs and meltdowns into moments of growth. It's gonna be an awesome journey, so grab your surfboard, and let's ride the waves together!

Here are detailed coping strategies that you can arm yourself with on the battlefield of parenting.

1. Breathing Exercises:

The simple yet powerful act of conscious breathing serves as the most effective method of coping with overwhelming emotions. Teach your child calming breathing exercises, such as deep belly breathing or counting breaths. This technique, easily accessible in moments of stress, anchors them in the present and promotes emotional regulation.

2. Mindfulness Practices:

Introduce age-appropriate mindfulness practices to cultivate a heightened awareness of the present moment. Activities like guided meditation or mindful coloring provide valuable tools for redirecting focus and promoting a sense of calm. These practices lay the groundwork for emotional resilience by fostering a non-judgmental awareness of thoughts and feelings.

3. Create a Relaxation Corner:

Designate a cozy corner in your home as a "relaxation corner." Fill it with soft pillows, calming colors, and sensory items like stress balls or textured fabrics. This designated space serves as a retreat where your child can retreat when feeling overwhelmed, engaging in calming activities to regain emotional balance.

4. Expressive Arts:

Encourage the use of expressive arts as a means of emotional expression and release. Whether through drawing, painting, or crafting, these creative outlets provide a non-verbal channel for children to externalize and process their emotions. The act of creation becomes a therapeutic journey, improving their emotional well-being.

5. Positive Affirmations:

Introduce the power of positive affirmations. Help your child create a list of affirmations that resonate with them, reinforcing positive self-talk. When faced with challenges, these affirmations become a reassuring mantra, instilling a sense of self-confidence and resilience.

Think of it like this: our brains are like gardens. When we plant positive seeds, like affirmations, they grow into blooming self-belief. But just like any garden, it needs nurturing. That's where you come in!

First, let's explore the science. Studies by Seligman et al. (1991) and Kernis et al. (2006) show that positive affirmations can actually boost optimism, self-esteem, and even academic performance. Pretty cool, right?

Now, onto the fun part: Creating affirmations with your child! Remember, these should be personal and meaningful to them. Here are some ideas to get you started:

For facing challenges: "I am brave and strong. I can overcome any obstacle!"

For managing emotions: "I can manage my feelings. I take deep breaths and stay calm."

For trying new things: "I am a learner. I am not afraid to make mistakes. I try my best and learn from them."

For self-compassion: "I am kind and loving to myself. I am perfect just the way I am."

Also, don't lose your magical touch: personalizing the affirmations! Let your child add their own superpowers, favorite colors, or anything that makes them feel special. For example, instead of "I am brave," it could be "I am as brave as Wonder Woman!"

6. Constructive Problem-Solving:

Teach your child constructive problem-solving skills. Guide them in breaking down challenges into manageable steps, fostering a proactive approach to difficulties. This coping strategy empowers them to face adversity with a mindset focused on solutions rather than being overwhelmed by the problem.

7. Physical Activity:

Engage in physical activities together as a family. Whether it's a nature walk, a playful game, or a dance session, physical activity releases endorphins, promoting a positive mood and serving as a natural coping mechanism for stress. This shared experience strengthens family bonds while nurturing emotional well-being.

8. Journaling:

Introduce the practice of journaling as a reflective tool. Encourage your child to jot down their thoughts, feelings, and experiences. This process not only provides an emotional outlet but also fosters self-awareness as they revisit their entries over time, recognizing patterns and growth.

9. Social Support Networks:

Encourage the importance of social connections and supportive relationships. Teach your child to reach out to trusted friends, family members, or teachers when they need emotional support. Building a network of understanding individuals reinforces the notion that seeking help is a strength, not a weakness.

10. Mindful Movement Practices:

Incorporate mindful movement practices such as yoga or tai chi into your child's routine. These activities combine physical movement with mindful awareness, promoting relaxation and enhancing emotional resilience. Engaging in these practices as a family further strengthens the bond while nurturing emotional well-being.

As we close this chapter on building emotional intelligence, remember: this isn't a checklist we complete and move on from. It's a lifelong tango with your child's emotions and your own. The tools we've explored—like identifying emotions, conquering tantrums, and fostering coping strategies—are just the first steps.

Think of them as the raw materials of the sculpture of your days. A playful "Guess the emotion game" during bath time. A deep breath together before tackling challenging homework. A story about a brave character who uses calming techniques to face their fears. These seemingly small moments stitch together a profound message: emotions are okay, and we have the tools to handle them.

This journey isn't always smooth. There will be tantrums, meltdowns, and moments of frustration. But just like any dance, practice makes perfect. And remember, you're not alone.

A small difference that you make is part of a larger movement, a collective effort to raise emotionally intelligent individuals who can fight the storms in life with grace and resilience. In a nutshell, know that you're building a stronger, more connected relationship with your child—a legacy that will resonate long after the final chapter is written.

Chapter 6: Games and Activities

Did you know that children learn best when they are having fun? This is where the power of games and activities comes in. They provide an engaging approach to teaching new ideas, reinforcing prior learning, and developing critical abilities in kids while maintaining their enthusiasm and motivation.

Imagine transforming a math lesson into a board game where children roll dice, add numbers, and strategize to win the game. Or picture a history lesson coming alive through a role-playing game where children reenact historical events, taking on different characters and voices. These are some examples of how games and activities can make learning a captivating experience.

The benefits go beyond mere engagement. Games cultivate collaboration and communication as children work together toward a common objective. They empower problem-solving and critical thinking as they explore challenges and make choices. Most importantly, they construct an adoration for learning, a sense of interest, and a desire to explore further.

So, the next time you're searching for ways to teach your child a valuable skill or lesson, grasp the control of play. By consolidating various activities, you will open a world of possibilities, turning learning into a pleasant and prosperous journey.

In the following tale, we will glimpse the transformative power of games and activities in parenting. Every hop, puppet dance, culinary creation, and bedtime story forms not just a fleeting moment but a stitch in the complex artwork of their life.

In a small, rural home lived a devoted father, Aaron, to his little muse, Blakeley. With a heart brimming with warmth, Aaron accepted the transformative control of games as a vehicle for conferring the significant lessons of life.

One sunny evening, as the golden beams sifted through the leaves, Aaron changed their backyard into an innovative garden of creative energy. Armed with colorful chalk, he drew a dynamic hopscotch grid that led Blakeley on a journey of numbers, balance, and giggles. Each jump carried a lesson—a numeral to memorize, a balance to master, and the sheer bliss of movement.

In this simple game, Aaron wasn't simply teaching how to count; he was refining Blakeley's motor skills, ingraining the significance of perseverance (particularly when attempting to bounce on one foot), and sowing the seeds of a deep-rooted love for physical action. The hopscotch network became a canvas where the conventional act of play could bloom into a showstopper of learning.

The father-daughter duo moved to the cozy limits of their living room. With a makeshift puppet theater crafted from an old shoebox and a sprinkle of imagination, Aaron and Blakeley set out on a creative storytelling journey.

Puppets danced, characters whispered tales of adventure, and lessons emerged as constellations in the night sky. In this unique way, Aaron bestowed values, sparked interest, and transported Blakeley to domains where imagination reigned. The puppet theater became a doorway to a world where stories weren't just amusement but vessels of intelligence and inspiration.

The next morning, the aroma of a delightful feast floated through the kitchen as the two wore matching aprons and prepared for their culinary adventure.

What began as an introductory baking session became a delightful experience of measurements, teamwork, and a sprinkle of flour-induced laughter.

As flour-covered hands worked in pairs, Aaron consistently integrated math lessons into the recipe.

"How many cups of flour do we need, Blakeley?" he inquired, turning the measuring cups into instruments of arithmetic exploration. Amid the floury chaos, a beautiful cake gradually rose to perfection.

"Daddy, we did it!" Blakeley excitedly clapped her hands. Little did she know that Aaron's real sense of accomplishment was the bunch of lessons woven into their shared kitchen adventures.

As the day drew to a close, Aaron settled into the role of a bedtime storyteller. The dim gleam of a bedside lamp changed their shared sleep-time routine into a trip through enchanting stories and meaningful conversations.

With each story, Aaron quietly implanted life lessons—values of benevolence, courage, and the magnificence of grasping uniqueness. Through the mysterious stories spun within the quietude, Aaron supported not only Blakeley's love for stories but also the values that would shape her character.

As we discover the avenues of games and activities in parenting, we also find that in the ordinary, there lies the extraordinary; in play, there's not just laughter but the seeds of lifelong learning and connection.

Unlocking Learning Through Play

As times have changed, there has been a quiet revolution in education, where instead of lectures and textbooks, games and activities have become powerful friends in the learning process. Gameplay is similar to parents hiding veggies in their kid's food, almost like sugarcoating the pill. Let's discuss the benefits of including engaging activities in the classroom as much more than simply a fun diversion.

1. Prolonged Engagement: One of the compelling reasons to blend gameplay in education is the unparalleled level of engagement they elicit. In contrast to conventional teaching approaches that could find it challenging to retain a child's interest, well-made games provide an engaging and exciting learning environment. This increased involvement creates an environment where education is no longer seen as a chore but as an adventure.

2. Making Learning Memorable: The human brain has an extraordinary capacity to retain information when it's embedded in memorable experiences. As games can move quickly, they require students to be alert and energetic for extended periods. Researchers at the University of Wisconsin in Madison found that games actually benefit students by helping them shape their attentiveness and training the brain in how to learn.

So, whether solving puzzles, participating in simulations, or engaging in hands-on experiments, each activity becomes a bookmark in the child's cognitive landscape—a vivid memory associated with knowledge gained.

3. Promoting Intrinsic Motivation: Motivation is the fuel that drives learning in education. Intrinsic motivation derived from personal interest and fulfillment may be uniquely tapped into by games and activities. Children who experience happiness and fulfillment in the learning process transform from being passive information consumers to active learners, which promotes greater comprehension and a lifelong thirst for knowledge.

4. Tailoring Learning to Individual Needs: Every child is unique and has different learning styles, preferences, and paces. Gameplay provides a versatile platform to alter education to individual needs. Whether a child thrives on visual stimuli, hands-on experiences, or collaborative endeavors, the diverse landscape of games allows parents to customize learning experiences, ensuring that every child has the opportunity to shine.

5. Encouraging Critical Thinking: Games are inherently structured around challenges and problem-solving, making them powerful tools for nurturing critical thinking skills. From strategic board games to interactive puzzles, these activities prompt children to analyze situations, make decisions, and adapt their approaches.

A study at the University of Manchester 2016 concluded that "Playing interactive educational games may have a positive impact on children's problem-solving skills and engage them in advanced mathematical thinking." The process of deciphering rules, anticipating outcomes, and strategizing fosters a robust framework for critical thinking and problem-solving skills that extend far beyond the game board.

6. Building Social Skills and Collaboration: Many games and activities are inherently social, encouraging collaboration, communication, and teamwork. Whether working together to solve a problem, negotiating rules, or strategizing as a team, these experiences cultivate essential social skills. In an era where social skills are as vital as academic knowledge, games become a dynamic avenue for honing these life skills.

As a parent, playing with your child can help strengthen your relationship, promote positive communication, and foster their cognitive, emotional, and social development. Additionally, playing together can be fun, bonding with each other and creating cherished memories. You may actually end up finding some shared interests with your little one, or at least you will get to understand their interests better.

7. Applying Learning to Real-world Contexts: The bridge between theoretical knowledge and real-world application can be fortified through games and activities. Simulations, role-playing, and scenario-based games immerse children in practical contexts, enabling them to apply theoretical concepts to real-life situations. This connection between learning and application lays the groundwork for a more comprehensive and meaningful understanding of the subject matter.

8. Elevating Emotional Intelligence: Emotional intelligence is developed through games and activities that frequently deal with emotional topics. Through various activities such as role-playing, storytelling, and teamwork, kids are exposed to a world where critical thinking, empathy, and effective communication are essential skills for learning. Playing games helps children develop emotional literacy, which gives them valuable life skills outside of the classroom.

Ada, an energetic middle-aged mom with eyes that sparkled like emeralds, trudged into the living room after a tough day at work. Her six-year-old son, Alaric, sat sprawled on the floor, clutching his favorite stuffed tiger, Bartholomew, with a tear rolling down his cheek.

"Alaric, what's wrong?" Ada inquired with concern.

With his lower lip trembling, Alaric mumbled something about Bartholomew being lost in the jungle during their imaginary safari adventure. Ada sighed and knelt beside him, her eyes mirroring his sadness. From researching about a million ways of parenting, Ada had resolved never to dismiss her son's emotions.

"Oh no, that's terrible," she said softly. "Bartholomew must be feeling scared, all alone in the jungle. How can we help him?"

Alaric sniffled and looked up at his mother with hope flickering in his eyes.

Together, they devised a plan. They grabbed blankets and pillows, changing the living room into a dense jungle. Crawling on all fours, they became explorers, braving the treacherous terrain, their voices hushed with the thrill of adventure.

Their journey led them through imaginary rivers, over precarious monkey bars, and finally, to a clearing where Bartholomew, abandoned beneath a pile of cushions, awaited them. Alaric's face lit up with relief as he scooped Bartholomew into his arms, showering him with imaginary hugs and kisses.

As they played, Ada didn't simply solve Alaric's problem; she acknowledged his emotions, validating his feelings of worry and loss. She then encouraged him to problem-solve, advancing his critical thinking and communication skills. They worked together, building empathy and understanding through their shared experience.

9. Elevating Education to an Enriching Experience: Gameplay provides children with a natural way to learn and develop. As much as games can be about instilling a concept, they're also about learning from what goes wrong. Play lets children practice what they know and also what they don't. It allows them to experiment through trial and error, find solutions to problems, work out the best strategies, and build new confidence and skills.

As Stanford researchers point out, kids learn to never abandon the game, even when they've lost. This not only encourages a growth mindset, but it also, in time, boosts self-esteem when the kids eventually correct their mistakes and receive praise.

Moreover, playing with your child helps model positive behaviors, such as taking turns, teamwork, and abiding by rules. They teach children how to be responsible and manage their time by learning to balance out their leisure time with their duties. So, what are you waiting for already? Dive right into the world of games and activities with your cupcake!

Why Patience is the Secret Weapon in Fun

Can you already imagine the allure of laughter echoing through the house as you play around with your kid? That twinkle of excitement in your child's eyes as they master a new skill, and the loud "Hurrah" as they succeed. The path to these dreams conjured by the world of games and activities is often paved with unexpected and unforeseen challenges. This is where the often-overlooked hero comes into light – patience.

You might ask, "Now, why do I need patience to let my baby have some fun?" Okay, then close your eyes and visualize seeing a big jigsaw puzzle scattered all across the floor the moment you step out of your room after a long day. Sound frustrating right? You just feel like throwing the complete puzzles away because seriously, "Why don't they ever put it back in place after playing?"

The frustration is real, but here's why shifting your thinking and summoning patience is incredibly important:

1. Understanding their world: To a child, it's not a mess—it's their ongoing project. A jigsaw puzzle is exploration; its pieces are full of wonder and possibility. They don't yet fully grasp the concept of "cleaning up" in the way we do.

Children, especially young ones, learn about the world through play. Dissecting a puzzle, even if that means leaving it in pieces, helps them understand how parts form a whole, developing their problem-solving skills and fine motor coordination.

2. Building Frustration Tolerance: While frustrating, allowing your child to understand the puzzle (and not immediately cleaning up after them) helps them build frustration tolerance. This is an essential life skill. They'll learn that not everything comes together immediately and that persistence is sometimes required. This will help them deal with bigger challenges later in life.

3. The Value of Effort over Outcome: Sometimes, it's okay for children not to complete a puzzle. By emphasizing the enjoyment of the process and minimizing the pressure of putting everything perfectly back together, you teach them an important lesson. Often, it's the effort and exploration we put into something that matters more than a 'perfect' result.

4. A model, not an opponent: Think about the long-term. Our reactions when children are young create a lasting impression. Impatience and frustration send a message that mistakes are intolerable. That can stifle their curiosity and confidence to try new things. Patience, on the other hand, shows that it's okay to take time to figure things out and that you are there to support them.

5. Relationship Building: It's hard to see in the heat of the moment, but patience builds a stronger bond. Kids feel discouraged when we fight against them. By taking a deep breath, helping them pick up a few pieces, and perhaps turning it into a game, you're working with them instead of against them. That's the groundwork for a trusting relationship.

6. Patience is a muscle: Each time you choose patience, even when it's tough, you strengthen that 'patience muscle' in your own brain. This benefits not just those frustrating puzzle moments but spills over into every area of life. It will help you manage future challenges in parenting and beyond with a more level head.

So, next time, instead of losing patience, try these few exercises:

Take a deep breath: When frustrations bubble up, take a moment to breathe deeply and center yourself. This will help you respond calmly and effectively to your child's needs.

Think long-term: Instead of stressing about the immediate mess, think of the skills your child is gaining and the person you are helping them become.

Offer guidance, not solutions: Instead of doing the puzzle for them, ask if they'd like some help figuring it out or suggest working on it together.

Set Realistic Expectations: Don't expect your child to master a concept or complete an activity flawlessly in the first attempt. Celebrate progress, not just perfection.

Focus on the Process, Not Just the End Result: Enjoy the laughter, the collaboration, and the joy of discovery. Don't get overly fixated on reaching the "finish line" of the activity.

Take Breaks: When you or your child feels overwhelmed, step away from the activity and come back to it later with fresh energy and enthusiasm.

Embrace the Unexpected: Play-based learning isn't necessarily linear, and unanticipated difficulties can occur. Accept them as chances for mutual learning and adaptation.

Patience might seem hard in the heat of the moment, but trust me—the rewards for both your child and your own sanity are immense! There will be moments when your little learner struggles to grasp a concept, gets frustrated with repeated attempts, or simply loses interest in the activity. These moments, though seemingly disruptive, are invaluable opportunities for growth.

By remaining calm and supportive, you create a safe space for your child to explore, experiment, and, ultimately, learn. This doesn't mean disregarding their struggles; instead, it's about acknowledging their emotions, offering guidance without judgment, and celebrating their small victories with genuine enthusiasm. Following are the key personality traits that you will instill in your child by putting on the cloak of patience.

1. Confidence: When you remain patient in the face of your child's struggles, you send a powerful message: "I believe in you, and I know you can do this." This unwavering belief builds confidence and a sense of self-efficacy in your child. They learn that perseverance is rewarded and that challenges are not insurmountable hurdles but stepping stones to mastery.

2. Curiosity: Your youngster can explore freely in a patient setting without worrying about being judged or failing. This encourages children to ask questions, try out various strategies, and learn new things on their own, which feeds their innate curiosity. It takes this internal drive to cultivate a lifetime love of learning.

3. Communication: Learning through play often involves nonverbal communication and shared experiences. By demonstrating patience, you encourage your child to express their thoughts and feelings openly. This creates an opportunity for deeper connection and allows you to tailor your support and guidance to their specific needs.

4. A Positive Learning Environment: Frustration and impatience can quickly turn a fun game into a stressful experience. By maintaining a positive and patient demeanor, you create a warm and inviting learning environment where your child feels comfortable taking risks, making mistakes, and learning from them.

5. Patience is Contagious: Children learn by observing and mimicking the behavior of those around them. By demonstrating patience, you offer your child a valuable life lesson—that patience is not a passive virtue but an active choice, one that leads to better problem-solving, frustration tolerance, and, ultimately, a happier and more fulfilling life.

Remember, the reward of witnessing your child's "aha" moment, the excitement in their eyes as they grasp a new concept, or the joy they experience during the learning process is worth the challenges. By embracing patience as your secret weapon, you can turn fun-filled learning into a transformative experience for you and your child.

Fun Ways to Teach Patience through Play

The struggle to keep children still and focused feels like an endless tug-of-war in today's world. Gone were the days of simple toys and quiet afternoons. The current generation, wired on a constant stream of fast-paced, brightly colored stimuli from screens, seemed to have an insatiable appetite for movement and instant gratification. Bet you agree! Let's learn from how Sasha tackles this harsh reality.

One afternoon, Sasha found herself refereeing a living room war between her two sons, Joe and Alan. Ten-year-old Joe, bouncing on the sofa like a human pogo stick, narrated his imaginary spaceship adventures at decibel levels that rivaled a jet engine. Seven-year-old Alan's eyes glued to his tablet swiped and tapped with a fervor that suggested he was single-handedly fighting an epic digital battle.

"Boys! Please, settle down for a bit," Sasha pleaded, her voice barely audible over the din. Joe paused mid-flight, momentarily distracted, before resuming his frenetic bouncing. Alan, however, remained oblivious, his brow furrowed in concentration.

Reaching her wit's end, Sasha decided on a different approach. "How about we play a game?" she suggested, her voice laced with a hint of playful enthusiasm. The word "game" piqued their interest. Joe, intrigued, hopped off the sofa while Alan, ever so slightly, lifted his gaze from the tablet.

She led them outside, where the afternoon sun was casting long shadows across the backyard. She pointed to a patch of soft grass. "This is our spaceship," she declared.

"Joe, you be the pilot, and Alan, you're the navigator. But remember, spaceships need fuel, and the only way to get it is to be calm and focused."

Intrigued, the boys settled down on the grass, their initial restlessness replaced by the novelty of the situation. Sasha continued, "To fuel the ship, we must take deep breaths together, slow and steady, just like the wind rustling through the leaves."

They practiced their deep breaths, the initial giggles fading as they found a rhythm. Slowly, the tension in their bodies eased, replaced by a sense of calm. With each breath, Sasha constructed stories of trudging along asteroid fields and encountering friendly alien creatures, all requiring quiet focus from her crew.

As the sun began to dip below the horizon, painting the sky in hues of orange and pink, the "spaceship" landed back in the backyard. Joe and Alan, no longer bouncing and swiping, helped Sasha gather fallen leaves, their faces flushed with the healthy glow of an afternoon spent playing, not just with their mother, but with their own imaginations.

The battle against hyperactivity may never be fully won, but Sasha had discovered that with a little creativity and a willingness to meet them on their terms, even the most tech-savvy generation could be engaged in a different kind of adventure, one that nurtured calm and connection.

According to the Royal Spanish Academy (RAE), patience is defined as: "The faculty of knowing how to wait when something is very much desired." Taking tips from Sasha's impromptu spaceship idea, all of us parents can also calm down our ever-active kids and make them utilize their energies constructively.

So, the next time your child is running around or perhaps throwing a fit when asked to leave their video game, instead of yelling, "Stop right now!" say, "Let's play a game!" And, of course, make sure to add that extra sparkle of enthusiasm in your eyes when you say that. Here is a list of some creative ways to teach the precious message of patience to your child:

1. The Waiting Game: Create a simple board game where players move forward spaces by demonstrating patience in various scenarios. Whether it's waiting for a turn on the swing or for the cookies to bake, infuse these moments with a sense of anticipation and excitement. Use simple countdowns or sing-along songs to make the act of waiting a shared and enjoyable experience. The first player to reach the finish line becomes the "Patience Champion."

2. Storytelling Relay: Organize a storytelling relay where each participant contributes a sentence to build a collective story. The catch? Participants must patiently wait their turn and build upon the narrative without interrupting. This fosters both patience and creativity.

3. Patience Jenga: Transform the classic Jenga game into a patience-building activity. Attach small challenges or questions to each Jenga block. Players must wait for their turn, pull a block, and complete the challenge before placing it on top.

4. Mindful Coloring: Provide intricate coloring sheets or mandalas for participants. Set a timer and encourage them to color mindfully, paying attention to each stroke. This not only promotes patience but also serves as a relaxing activity while instilling an appreciation of beauty in your child.

5. Puzzle Race: Choose a challenging puzzle and divide participants into teams. Each team must work together patiently to complete the puzzle. The catch is that the team must wait for their turn to place a piece, promoting collaboration and patience.

6. Garden Planting: Engage participants in a gardening activity. Planting seeds, tending to plants, and eagerly awaiting the first sprouts teach children the art of nurturing and waiting for growth. The anticipation of seeing a tiny seed transform into a blooming flower instills a sense of patience and responsibility.

7. Memory Card Game: Create a memory card game where players match pairs of cards with images related to patience, such as a clock, a turtle, or someone waiting in line. This not only enhances memory but also subtly reinforces the theme of patience.

8. Impulse Control Freeze Dance: Host a freeze dance party where participants dance freely to music. When the music stops, they must freeze immediately. This game teaches impulse control and the ability to wait for the cue before taking action.

9. DIY Board Game Design: Encourage participants to design their own board games that incorporate patience-related challenges. This sparks creativity and allows them to think critically about how to infuse the concept of patience into a game.

10. Patience Charades: Create a charades game with scenarios that require patience. Participants act out situations like waiting for a bus, standing in a long queue, or patiently listening to a friend. It's a fun and interactive way to reinforce the importance of patience.

11. Balloon Breathing: Incorporate a breathing exercise into a balloon-themed activity. Participants must inflate and deflate balloons slowly, syncing their breath with the balloon's movements. It teaches patience and mindfulness in a playful manner.

12. The Patience Jar: Introduce a "Patience Jar" where participants contribute notes describing situations where they demonstrated patience or observed it in others. Periodically, read and discuss these stories to reinforce the positive aspects of patience.

13. Building Block Challenge: Provide building blocks or construction sets and ask participants to construct a structure collaboratively. They must take turns placing blocks, fostering patience, teamwork, and creativity.

14. Patience Puzzles: Select puzzles with varying difficulty levels. Participants can choose a puzzle based on their patience threshold. As they progress through more intricate puzzles, they learn the value of persistence and patience.

15. Role-Playing Scenarios: Create role-playing scenarios where participants act out situations that require patience, such as waiting for a friend who is running late or dealing with a slow internet connection. This interactive activity enhances empathy and patience.

16. Stories of patient animals: Don't we all, especially our young ones, simply love a good story?

Why don't you take advantage of that? Tell them stories of:

- **Spiders** painstakingly build their webs to capture insects and obtain food.

- **Snails** who seal themselves inside their shells when the air isn't right and calmly wait for the humidity in the surrounding air to increase.

- **Bears** that must hibernate for extended periods of time in order to withstand the bitter cold; otherwise, they would freeze to death.

- **Ants** patiently follow the paths for hours to bring the leaves and sticks needed to build their tiny home, so it takes them a very long time to build their nests.

17. Origami: Although the method of folding paper to make figures is very old, it is still widely used, enjoyable, and easy to execute. Children practice hand skills and fine motor abilities with this game, in addition to acquiring patience and concentration.

18. Egg Races: A classic game you can do at home, it's fun and great for kids to learn patience.

The process is simple:

1. Set up a course with a start and finish line.

2. Give a large spoon to each participant.

3. Place a boiled egg on each spoon.

4. The children must complete the course without the egg falling off the spoon.

5. The winner is the one who arrives first with the unbroken egg in the utensil!

19. Nature's Time Capsule: This is a nature scavenger hunt but with a twist. Instead of swiftly collecting items, designate a special "nature's time capsule" spot. As children find treasures, they can add them to the capsule, fostering the idea that sometimes the joy lies in patiently curating a collection.

20. Obstacle Course Overture: Design an obstacle course that intertwines physical activity with patience. Whether it's balancing on a line, waiting for a partner to complete a section, or navigating challenges, the course becomes a playful arena for learning the art of waiting.

21. Game of Reflection: After an exciting day of play, gather for a reflective session. Discuss the favorite moments, challenges faced, and how patience played a role. Encourage children to express their feelings, reinforcing the idea that patience is a valuable asset in navigating both play and life.

22. Collaborative Art Gallery: Create a collaborative art gallery within the home. As each family member contributes their artistic pieces, the gallery evolves. This ongoing project teaches the importance of patience, shared creativity, and the beauty of patiently waiting for a masterpiece to unfold.

23. Rock Garden Storytime: Craft a rock garden together, where each rock represents a special moment or achievement. Whether waiting for the glue to dry or deciding on the perfect arrangement, this activity weaves patience into creating a tangible memory garden.

24. Starry Night Stargazing: On clear evenings, engage in stargazing as a family. This simple yet profound activity encourages children to patiently observe the night sky, sparking curiosity and nurturing a sense of wonder that unfolds gradually.

These activities go beyond mere amusement—they serve as a springboard for cultivating patience in a playful yet profound way. Whether it's the strategic planning of a board game, the intense focus of a creative challenge, or the teamwork involved in a shared project, these experiences impart valuable lessons in patience while having a blast. Participants not only have a great time but also acquire essential life skills in a fun and engaging manner.

The creak of the swing set echoed in the sleepy afternoon as Polly pushed Ty higher and higher. He squealed with delight, his small hand gripping the chains tightly. Ty, six years old and new to the neighborhood, had a quiet shyness about him.

Polly, a single mother, had become a self-proclaimed "fun director" for her introverted son. Games became their daily ritual: building forts from blankets, crafting imaginary worlds with sticks and stones, or staging epic battles with water balloons. Polly's infectious enthusiasm drew Ty out of his shell. He learned to laugh, to collaborate, and, most importantly, to trust.

As they grew, their games evolved. Polly, a natural storyteller, would create brilliant stories during their pretend play. Ty, captivated by her words, would add details, his voice gaining confidence with each new adventure. This ignited his love for language, a skill he later blossomed in writing.

One rainy day, they discovered a dusty chessboard in the attic. Polly, never one to back down from a challenge, taught him the game.

"Think ahead, Ty," she'd say, her brow furrowed in concentration. Their battles were fierce, but through them, Ty learned the value of strategic thinking, a skill that would come in handy on the high school debate team.

Their shared love for games extended beyond their backyard. They'd spend summers huddled around the kitchen table, piecing together difficult puzzles. As the pieces clicked into place, so did their understanding of the bigger picture, a valuable skill in the science club Ty later joined.

Years passed, filled with laughter, shared secrets, and countless adventures. Polly helped Ty blossom into a confident young man. He learned the joy of collaboration, the power of storytelling, and the importance of strategic thinking, all through the games they shared.

As Ty stood on the podium, receiving an award for his environmental project, he looked out at the crowd. His gaze met Polly's, a silent exchange of gratitude passing between them. His mother had curated him into the person he had grown up to be. All those fun activities that they did together not only helped strengthen the bond between the mother and son but also made parenting a wholesome experience for Polly.

So remember, the best times are often the simplest. The next time you're looking for some joyful moments with your kid, ditch the screens and grab some balloons, sidewalk chalk, or even just use your silly voices! These games and activities are more than just fun; they're a chance to bond, unleash your inner child, and create memories that will last a lifetime. So get out there, play, and watch the laughter light up your world!

Chapter 7: Storytelling for Patience

Once upon a time, in the whimsical village of Flustered Fantasies, nestled amongst towering trees and tear-stained rivers, resided a weary parent named Elara. Her days were an unending routine of spilled milk tantrums and ear-splitting lullabies sung off-key. Elara's drooping eyelids longed for a moment of quiet, a reprieve from the relentless demands of her little one, Pip.

One particularly trying day, as Elara chased Pip through a mess of scattered toys, she noticed a shimmer of light flickering at the window. A tiny, effervescent fairy with wings like dandelion fluff perched on the windowsill. Her voice, a tinkling melody, offered, "Elara, here is the cure to your frustration. Take this book and see your life change magically."

The fairy handed Elara a book titled "Nurturing Patience." As she opened its pages, swirling stardust danced within, weaving tales of calm whispers and playful cooing. Slowly, as Elara devoured the book's wisdom, a transformation unfolded.

Instead of shouting over Pip's cries, Elara learned the calming magic of a patient embrace. When Pip refused vegetables, stories of brave knights battling broccoli foes piqued her interest. The once frantic days transformed into an exploration of giggles and shared discoveries.

Elara, no longer burdened by the weight of frustration, felt a lightness bloom within. Pip mirrored her calm demeanor and gradually became a curious adventurer as their bond deepened with each passing day. Their house, once shrouded in storm clouds of tension, began to bask in the warm glow of laughter and love.

The news of the magical book spread like dandelion seeds in the wind. Parents, rejuvenated by its wisdom, discovered the joy hidden within the chaos. And so, "Nurturing Patience" became a treasured heirloom, passed down through generations, a reminder that the magic of parenthood lies not in control but in the embrace of love, understanding, and a sprinkle of fairy-touched patience.

Well, considering that you have reached this far, you have already benefitted from half of the magic withheld in the book. Elara is you, Flustered Fantasies is your home, and Pip is your little storm of joy in your world. Did you like how enchantingly I created a story on the struggles of parents in today's world? Did it bring a smile to your face? What if I tell you that by the end of this chapter, you will have such fantasy tales at your fingertips, and they will clear the momentary dark clouds and show you a beautiful rainbow? Interested? Let's dive right in, then.

What was your favorite story when you were growing up? Was it a traditional fairy tale like *Rapunzel* or *Little Red Riding Hood*? Or was it picture books like *Charlie and the Chocolate Factory* and *Chronicles of Narnia*? Let's not forget the legendary JK Rowling's *Harry Potter*!

Think about how your favorite story made you feel. Did you learn anything from it? Did it make you behave or think differently? A study published in the Journal of Developmental Psychology found that children who listened to stories about helpful characters were more likely to help out in a subsequent scenario compared to those who listened to neutral stories. This suggests that stories can not only entertain but also shape children's moral development and guide their behavior in positive ways.

Growing up, bedtime stories whispered in the dark were like a portal to a world where we were the main character, where we could be anyone we wanted to be and do anything we wanted to do. As our parents read stories of princesses with golden hair and wise animals that talked, our imagination was built gradually, one step at a time. The line between reality and imagination blurred, fueled by tales of bravery, magic, and creatures both terrifying and delightful.

For many of us, sharing and reading stories was an important part of our childhood, superior to the world of distracting screens and 24/7 streaming. I'm sure you would agree that life just isn't as simple anymore. And before you blame screens, think about this: When was the last time you heard a parent telling a story to their child?

A 2018 research study found that nowadays, only 30% of parents read to their children daily. It is paradoxical how we emphasize the phrase "communication is key" in personal relationships and business dealings, yet we turn a blind eye to its importance in nurturing a child's tender mind.

You have to understand that communication in parenting is fundamentally different from communication between adults. Unlike adults, children cannot simply sit and absorb a list of instructions or explanations. Their developing brains, while full of potential and curiosity, are also delicate and require a gentler approach. To bridge the gap between your adult perspective and your child's unique way of understanding the world, storytelling emerges as a powerful tool. Through imaginative narratives, you can nourish their minds and subtly convey your message in a way that resonates with their cognitive development.

In the fast-paced world of today, it is easy to get caught up in the race to provide our children with everything they need to succeed, but we tend to miss the simplest things that have the biggest impact on their growth and development.

Imagine a scene where a parent sits down with their child and sets out on an adventure through words. As they dive further into the story, the child's eyes widen with wonder, their imagination flowing with every vivid description. They get transported to distant lands, meet fascinating characters, and learn the beauty of resilience, kindness, and bravery. In that moment, a connection is forged—a bridge between the past and the future, between generations.

Storytelling is the oldest form of communication known to man, our own way to share experiences, connect with others and learn new things. And who doesn't love a good story? There is just something about stories that can captivate us, help us cope, and make us feel connected to the characters and to each other. Be it a book or a TV show on Netflix, a good tale is ideal for comfort, entertainment, and escaping the harsh reality of the world.

The Magic Of Stories

The benefits of storytelling extend far beyond childhood. It has a regulating effect on the nervous systems of both the listener and the teller. Unlike other entertainers, the job of a storyteller is to disappear and let the story do the work. They have to slow down, become present, absorb the words of the story, imagine all the details, and lose themselves in them. They have to create the experience of magic so that when the story is over, children heave a sigh of satisfaction. It is an exhilarating feeling, not the caffeinated kind, but the steady hum that you get from meditation or yoga.

Storytelling is a powerful tool that goes beyond imparting the value of books; it actively contributes to a child's early literacy skills and brain development. Through the enchanting world of stories, children not only get to know sounds and words but also cultivate the ability to focus. Reading stories in their native tongue aids effective communication, helping kids familiarize themselves with different letters, syllables, and sounds in their language.

Furthermore, storytelling becomes a multifaceted catalyst for social, communication, and emotional skill development. It serves as a gateway for children to learn about the world and their culture, fostering a sense of self and an understanding of their surroundings. For preschoolers, stories play a pivotal role in helping them make sense of their thoughts and emotions and navigate social expectations in different settings.

Engaging narratives that introduce challenges resolved over time contribute to the development of longer-term problem-solving skills. As children listen to stories, they not only enjoy the tales but also begin to articulate their own play, learning how to craft and tell stories with enthusiasm.

Simple stories featuring rhymes, songs, and repetition become linguistic stepping stones, familiarizing children with language patterns and allowing them to recognize parts of the story. This early exposure improves language and vocabulary, laying the foundation for a lifelong love of reading. Additionally, storytelling nurtures imagination, creative thinking, and self-confidence, providing comfort to children during times of change and uncertainty through familiar characters and beloved tales.

Moreover, stories become invaluable tools for addressing difficult topics. Whether discussing the loss of a close relative or navigating the complexities of family dynamics, storytelling provides a gentle opening for adults to guide discussions on tricky behaviors or emotions.

In the midst of the chaos of daily life, sharing a story creates a precious moment for calm and contemplation. It offers a delightful break, allowing both children and adults to immerse themselves in the magic of storytelling, forging connections, and building a foundation for a lifelong appreciation of literature.

Storytelling is a powerful tool to help children understand their health experiences. It can help them feel less alone, ease their fears, and give them hope. So, next time you are faced with a health scare, reach for a story. It just might be the best medicine for what ails you. Here is a breakdown of the benefits of storytelling in parenting:

1. Building Bridges of Connection: Storytelling serves as an invisible bridge connecting hearts. Through tales of their own challenges, triumphs, and moments of vulnerability, parents invite children into a shared space of understanding, fostering an emotional bond that withstands the test of time. When families talk about their past experiences together, it brings them closer and helps maintain emotional bonds.

2. Teach Values: Parents can craft tales that subtly convey moral lessons, ethical principles, and the importance of empathy. By presenting characters who grapple with dilemmas or exhibit kindness, parents instill values organically, allowing children to absorb these lessons through the engaging medium of storytelling.

A study about family storytelling found that "Family stories provide a sense of identity through time and help children understand who they are in the world." Researchers discovered that when parents told family stories to their kids, the kids tended to think more highly of their families, had higher self-esteem, showed less anxiety, had fewer behavioral issues, and were better equipped to handle stress.

3. Navigating Complex Emotions: Stories act as compasses guiding children through the intricate terrain of emotions. Whether it's characters steering friendship, coping with loss, or overcoming fears, stories provide a safe space for children to explore and understand their own feelings. Through these narratives, parents impart emotional intelligence, equipping children with the tools to navigate the rich tapestry of their inner worlds.

4. Encouraging Imagination and Creativity: Storytelling sparks the flames of imagination, inviting children into realms where the ordinary meets the extraordinary. As parents weave tales of fantastical adventures or everyday heroes, they nurture a child's creativity and curiosity. This imaginative play not only enhances cognitive development but also lays the foundation for a lifelong appreciation for storytelling in various forms.

Through characters, plots, and settings, children engage in mental exercises that enhance critical thinking, problem-solving, and comprehension skills.

This cognitive workout within the realms of storytelling lays the foundation for academic success and lifelong learning.

Studies also show that when parents used more details and emotions when discussing past everyday events, called elaborative reminiscing, their children told more detailed and coherent narratives one to two years later. These children also demonstrated a better understanding of other people's thoughts and emotions.

5. Teach Life Skills: Beyond academic lessons, stories become vessels for imparting practical life skills. Parents can craft narratives that address decision-making, problem-solving, and interpersonal dynamics. Through relatable characters facing real-world scenarios, children absorb these skills organically, preparing them for the complexities of adulthood.

6. Facing Transitions and Milestones: As children traverse the landscape of growth, storytelling becomes a guide through transitions and milestones. Whether it's starting school, dealing with change, or approaching adolescence, stories provide descriptions that mirror and illuminate these life phases. Through thoughtful storytelling, parents assist children in navigating uncertainties with resilience and understanding.

7. Fostering a Love for Learning: Storytelling becomes a gateway to the vast realm of knowledge and learning. Parents can introduce historical events, scientific discoveries, or cultural richness through captivating narratives. By intertwining education with storytelling, parents cultivate a love for learning that extends beyond the structured confines of classrooms.

8. Passing down Family Legacies: Every family, no matter their background or situation, has a tale to tell. Even stories about the more trying times in life might teach kids something. Children who have personal family histories learn more about their origins and identity while also developing an interest in history. It's also a significant means of transmitting a family's history.

Stories become bridges connecting children to diverse cultures, traditions, and perspectives. By sharing stories from various cultural backgrounds, parents broaden their children's understanding of the world. This cultural exposure nurtures acceptance, tolerance, and an appreciation for the rich diversity that colors our global world.

9. Build Language Skills: By immersing children in rich storytelling, parents contribute to the development of language skills. From expanding vocabulary to understanding sentence structures, stories become linguistic playgrounds where children explore the nuances of expression.

10. Creating Lasting Memories: Storytelling becomes a treasure trove of cherished memories. From bedtime tales to family anecdotes, these shared stories become the cornerstone of lasting memories. As children reminisce about the characters, lessons, and shared laughter within these narratives, they carry forward a legacy of storytelling that spans generations.

In the enchanting alchemy of storytelling, parents gift their children with more than words on a page; they bestow a legacy of learning, understanding, and shared adventures. The benefits harvested from these literary odysseys reverberate far beyond childhood, shaping individuals who carry the magic of storytelling in their hearts—a timeless gift that transcends the pages of any book.

How to start Storytelling?

It is quite simple, actually. Just make up stories on the spot. You may feel that you need to have a plan, a great deal of preparation, and even practice for telling a bedtime story. To be honest, I discourage that. It doesn't just ruin the thrill of impromptu tales, but it also wears you out over time. Instead, I recommend sitting down and beginning with a "Once upon a time," and then letting your flow of thoughts make up the most bizarre story ever. Trust me, a disorganized and weird story is the best one of all!

"Inside each of us is a natural-born storyteller, waiting to be released."

- Robin Moore

For some of you, this may seem stressful and risky. You might find it difficult to create stories out of your imagination. Well, here is a powerful tip: look around the room, pick any small random thing, and start your story with it. Teddy bear? Tell a story about a bear. See a cracked window? Tell a story about a haunted house. Sound of creaking floorboards? Tell a story about a detective and a missing clue. With practice, this will become easier and a ton of fun for you and your listener.

If you still feel overwhelmed, here are some ideas to get you started with room for your child's creativity:

Everyday objects come to life: Turn a trip to the grocery store into an adventure. Perhaps the apples are having a meeting about the best way to be eaten, or the carrots are on a daring escape from the chopping block!

What-if scenarios: Start with a question like "What if your stuffed animals could talk?" or "What if your bed could fly?" Let your child take the lead in imagining the fantastical situations that arise.

Finish the story: Read a short story together that stops before the resolution. Brainstorm different endings together, silly or serious.

Draw and tell: Draw a picture together and then take turns narrating a story based on the image. You can add details as you go, making the story unfold together.

Classic themes, new twists: Use familiar fairy tale tropes like a brave hero or a hidden treasure but put a unique spin on them. Maybe the hero is afraid of heights, or the treasure turns out to be a pile of mismatched socks!

Remember, the key is to have fun and be creative. Embrace the silliness and let your child's imagination guide the story. The point is to lower your standards and remember that a poorly told story is better than none at all!

Coming to the question, when is the right time to tell stories? If you ask me, I think you can tell stories anytime. Be it bedtime, bath time, in the car, in the park, or on a dentist's visit—any time is a good time for a story! Make story time a part of your daily routine, either by carrying books around with you or by just using your mind.

Knowing when to stop can be just as important as finding the time to share a story in the first place. Pay attention to your child's reaction to the story, and stop if your child isn't enjoying it. You can always try a different book or story another time.

Some More Helpful Tips

- Use your voice to convey emotions in the story. You can do this by whispering or raising your voice and playing with the pitch of your voice (high for surprise and low for seriousness).

- Make a routine, and try to share at least one story every day. Create a special space where you and your child can go to read with a box of books and something comfortable to sit on.

- Use gestures, facial expressions, funny voices, noises, and so on. This can get your child interested and help them learn the meaning of words. It also makes it fun!

- Encourage your child to talk about the pictures and repeat familiar words and phrases.

- Make connections between your child's life and the book. For example, 'That little boy likes playing in the park, just like you!'

- Use props to help bring the story to life. This is extremely important for the young ones! These transitional objects can provide a sense of comfort to your child as they help them make the connection between the story and their own health experience.

- Include repeated phrases and rhymes from stories that they are familiar with. This helps them participate and retains interest. An example of a phrase from the Three Little Pigs is "I'll huff and I'll puff and I'll blow your house down!"

- You can build your stories on traditional ones. Try adding your kid's name in stories like *Cinderella*,

Aladdin, The Little Mermaid, or even *Bob the Builder.*

- Don't limit yourself to fiction because drawing stories from your personal experiences can be a great source of inspiration and fun!

- Use story prompts as a starting point. There are many resources available online, so just roll a dice and begin your story with prompts like "After being struck by lightning…"

- Encourage your child to ask questions and express their feelings about the story—this is an important part of the process and will help you gauge how well the story is helping your child cope.

Don't forget to enjoy the process yourself!

Choosing Appropriate Stories for Children

Stories are the cornerstones of childhood, opening doors to imagination and shaping young minds. But with countless books lining the shelves, selecting the most appropriate stories for a child can feel overwhelming. Here is a guide to selecting the right books/stories to tell your child:

1. Tailoring to Developmental Stage: Just as a skilled artist adjusts their technique to suit the canvas, parents must tailor storytelling to meet the cognitive, emotional, and linguistic needs of their child. For toddlers, simple narratives with vibrant images cater to burgeoning comprehension, while older children may crave more intricate plots and nuanced characters. Let me take you on a walk through the patterns that you will notice in the storytelling of your child. I have also added book recommendations as per the age.

Babies From Birth

Throughout their first year, babies' interactions with books evolve alongside their development. In the first 3 months, your baby might enjoy sitting on your lap and gazing at the pictures while you slowly read aloud. Your baby might pay attention to the book for only a few minutes.

By 9 months, your baby will start to engage more directly with the words and pictures in books. For example, your baby might babble while looking at pictures or try to lift up flaps. By 12 months, your baby will love being involved in storytime. Your baby can turn the book the right way up, point to pictures, and make animal noises or car and truck sounds. Your baby might even enjoy looking at books by themselves.

Follow your baby's lead, read slowly, and spend time looking at the pictures after you read the words. This lets your baby focus on the sounds and shapes of words and also on pictures. Turn the pages slowly when you read with your baby. This shows your baby how to use a book. Point out, name, and talk about familiar and new things your baby sees on the page instead of only reading the words. For example, 'That's a bunny.

Look. The bunny is hopping away'. Change the tone of your voice as you read. This makes it easier for your baby to notice different speech sounds, which is an important step toward learning to talk.

In general, babies enjoy and benefit from books that have good rhymes, regular rhythm, and repetition. Rhymes, rhythm, and repetition emphasize the way words sound, which helps with language development.

From when your baby is born, you might like to look for books that:

- Have bright colors or simple, large, and high-contrast pictures. These help grab their interest.

- Have different textures so your baby can hear, see, and feel the book.

- Have pictures of babies and faces.

- Are made of stiff cardboard and have only a few pages. They are easy for babies to hold and handle.

- Have themes that babies can relate to, like books about bathing, feeding, playing, and spending time outside.

Toddlers (12-18 months)

At this age, reading with your toddler is all about having fun with books, spending special time together, and learning. For example, your toddler will be picking new words as you read and look at pictures together. They might point to familiar objects in pictures and name them. They might say 'Shoe shoe' while pointing to a picture of a shoe. Or your toddler might make animal noises when they see pictures of animals or engine noises when they see pictures of cars or trucks.

Get your toddler to hold the book and help turn the pages. Ask your toddler to point to pictures. For example, 'Where's the puppy?' Build on your toddler's love for a favorite book by offering to read it regularly, as well as offering new or different books.

Toddlers often enjoy books with rhyme, rhythm, and repetition. Rhyme, rhythm, and repetition encourage your toddler to join in, which helps them learn. Your toddler's interests will guide you when you're choosing new books. You can understand what they like as you spend time and read with them.

At about 12 months, you could try the following types of books:

- Books about food, transport, animals, and other babies and toddlers

- Board books, which are easy to handle and very sturdy

- books that have pictures or illustrations of simple, familiar objects

- Lift-the-flap books with hidden items in each picture for your toddler to find

- Books with textures like fabric or collages in the illustrations

- Books about different cultures or books that show cultural diversity.

Toddler (18 months-3 years)

At this age, reading with your toddler is all about having fun with books, spending special time together, and modeling a love of books and reading. Help your toddler choose a book, and then ask them to hold the book and turn the pages. Read books like *Where is the Green Sheep?* which has repetitive words and phrases.

Repeat familiar words and phrases, and then get your toddler to fill in the words in familiar stories. Or try pausing and letting your toddler finish sentences for you – for example, 'Kitty said...?'

Ask your toddler to name, describe, or act out what they see on the page. For example, 'What's that? That's right – it's a monkey. What is the monkey doing? Can you jump up and down like that monkey?'

Toddlers often enjoy books that have good rhyme, rhythm, and repetition, and these qualities can help toddlers learn. Books that are the right length for your toddler can keep them engaged. Books that you can read in 4-5 minutes are usually a good length for toddlers.

Toddlers might especially enjoy:

- Simple stories with a beginning, middle, and end

- Books with animals and animal noises

- Books about a favorite topic, like cars, trucks, fairies, pets, stars and planets, music, castles, the ocean, princesses or trains

- Books about playtime that relate to their experiences

- Lift-the-flap and pop-up books—toddlers can have fun with books with moveable pieces.

Preschoolers

It's best to follow your child's lead with reading at this age. Sometimes your child will want to talk about the words and pictures, and sometimes they'll want to listen quietly while you read. At other times, your child might enjoy 'pretend reading' – that is, turning the pages and telling the story themselves.

Here are tips that can help you and your child make the most of your reading time.

Looking at the Book

Before you start, ask your child some questions about the book:

What do you think this story is about?

Who might be in it?

What do you think will happen?

Reading the Story

Vary the pace of your reading, as well as how loud you read. Changing your voice and expression for different characters and using gestures can also be fun.

Ask your child some questions about the story. For example, 'What do you think happens next?', 'Why is the baby happy?' or 'Who has the ball?'

Ask your child questions that help them relate to the story. For example, 'How would you feel if this was you?' or 'What would you do if this happened to you?'

Chant or sing repetitive phrases and words together. For example, "I'll knock, and I'll wait, and we'll find a friendly way!"

Add information when your child asks a question. For example, your child might point to a bear and ask, 'What's that?' You could say, 'That's a bear. It's sleeping in its cave because it is wintertime'.

Looking at Letters and Words

Older preschoolers might start to notice letters. For example, they might notice the letter that starts their name. Here are ways to build on this interest:

Point out the differences between letters and words and the difference between a lower-case and capital letter. For example, 'There is a capital S. Can you see how it's bigger than this lowercase s?'

When you see words printed in bold or large font, point these out and explain how this changes the way we say those words. For example, 'Look at how big the word BOOHOO is. The baby must be crying very loudly'. Ask questions about the names and sounds of letters. Play 'find the letters and words' games, especially with the letters in your child's name. Make sure to explain the meaning of any unusual words.

Other reading activities

Help your child make up stories and drawings to go with them. Make a storybook together. Let your child choose the story or use your child's own made-up stories and drawings. If your child can't read words, encourage your child to tell you a story based on the pictures in a book.

Avoid Sensitive Themes: There's a fascinating synergy between storytelling and brain development in children. Here's how stories influence a child's ethical compass:

Mirror Neurons and Empathy: Our brains contain mirror neurons, which fire when we witness actions or emotions. When children hear stories about characters experiencing kindness, these mirror neurons fire, creating a sense of empathy. This repeated exposure helps build empathy circuits in the brain, making it more natural for children to act kindly themselves.

Moral Reasoning and Story Frameworks: Stories provide a safe space for children to explore complex concepts like fairness, honesty, and helping others. By following the narrative arc of a story, children are unconsciously absorbing the cause-and-effect of ethical choices. This repetitive exposure helps develop their moral reasoning skills.

Social Learning and Role Models: Stories often present characters as role models. Children, especially in their early years, are highly observant and learn through imitation. By seeing characters exhibit positive ethical behaviors, children are more likely to integrate those behaviors into their own actions.

In essence, stories act as a powerful training ground for a child's developing ethical compass. By choosing stories that emphasize kindness, resilience, diversity, and empathy, parents can provide valuable guidance that shapes their child's moral foundation.

3. Cultural Relevance and Diversity: Stories are like a kaleidoscope—full of color and surprises! They come from everywhere, each one showing a different piece of the world. Reading these stories helps kids learn about different cultures and ways of life, making them more open-minded and understanding. It's like adding more colors to their own picture of the world!

4. Aligning with Interests: Just as a well-chosen melody resonates with the listener's heart, stories that align with a child's interests create a harmonious connection. Whether it's tales of adventure, animals, fantasy, or real-life heroes, weaving narratives around a child's passions ensures engagement and enthusiasm. These stories become not just lessons but enchanting journeys tailored to captivate young imaginations.

5. Promoting Inclusivity: The characters within stories become companions in a child's imaginative world. Choosing narratives that embrace inclusivity ensures that every child can see themselves reflected in the pages of a story. Inclusive storytelling celebrates diversity in race, abilities, family structures, and experiences, fostering a sense of belonging and acceptance.

6. Encouraging Active Participation: The magic of storytelling lies not just in the words spoken but in the dialogues it sparks. Appropriate stories invite active participation, encouraging children to ask questions, share their thoughts, and make connections to their own experiences. This interactive engagement transforms storytelling into a dynamic dialogue, enhancing comprehension and critical thinking.

7. Considering Emotional Sensitivity: Just as a gentle touch is needed for delicate brushstrokes, stories must be chosen with emotional sensitivity. Topics such as loss, fear, or friendship require thoughtful consideration. Parents navigate this delicate terrain by choosing stories that address emotions with empathy, offering a safe space for children to explore and understand their feelings.

8. Introducing Humor and Playfulness: Laughter and joy become the hues that infuse vibrancy into the canvas of storytelling. Appropriately incorporating humor and playfulness into stories adds a layer of delight. Whether through amusing characters, whimsical scenarios, or clever wordplay, these stories create moments of shared laughter that become cherished memories.

9. Encountering Life's Milestones: As children journey through the milestones of life, stories become trusted companions, guiding them through transitions. Appropriate stories can address experiences like starting school, making friends, or dealing with change. These narratives serve as beacons, offering comfort and insights during growth and uncertainty.

10. Embracing Diverse Formats: Stories don't solely reside within the pages of books; they manifest in various formats. Appropriate storytelling extends beyond traditional narratives, including audiobooks, interactive apps, and animated tales. Embracing diverse formats ensures that storytelling adapts to the evolving landscape of technology while maintaining its timeless essence.

In the artful selection of stories, parents wield a brush that paints not only pictures in a child's mind but also shapes their character. The stories chosen become stepping stones in a child's journey of understanding, empathy, and self-discovery. As parents carefully curate this literary landscape, they not only share tales but also lay the foundation for a lifelong love affair with the art of storytelling.

In a cozy corner of the old bookstore sat May and her son, Kai. May, with a warm smile, began weaving a tale. It was a story filled with brave knights battling fearsome dragons, a tale meant to spark Kai's adventurous spirit.

At first, Kai's eyes sparkled with excitement. He imagined himself as the knight, sword in hand, facing the monstrous dragon. However, as the story progressed, the details turned gruesome - the dragon's fiery breath and the knights' gruesome injuries. Kai, his face scrunched up in fear, shrank closer to his mother. The spark in his eyes had been replaced by tears.

Sensing his distress, May quickly altered the narrative. The battle didn't involve bloodshed. Instead, the knight outsmarted the dragon, using his wit and courage to find a peaceful solution. Kai's tears subsided, replaced by a relieved sigh. His imagination took flight again, this time painting a picture of bravery and cleverness.

That night, as Kai lay in bed, his mind replayed the altered story. He dreamt not of terrifying battles but of using his intelligence to overcome challenges. This gentle nudge in the storytelling direction, choosing a tale that resonated with his age and emotional growth, had a profound impact.

The next day, May visited the librarian, seeking guidance on selecting stories for Kai. The librarian explained, "Stories are like seeds. They plant ideas and emotions in young minds. Choosing the right ones, age-appropriate and positive, nurtures their imagination, shapes their values, and fosters emotional well-being."

With newfound understanding, May embarked on a journey of creating a safe and inspiring story world for Kai. She continued reading him tales, but now, with a keen eye for content. She sought stories that celebrated kindness, courage, and resilience, avoiding those filled with excessive violence or negativity.

As Kai grew, so did his love for stories. He learned not just about imaginary worlds but also about important life lessons. He discovered the power of empathy from the tale of the little mouse who helped a lion and the importance of perseverance from the story of the tortoise who beat the hare.

Years later, while browsing the same bookstore, Kai, now a young adult, came across a book on hero archetypes. He picked it up, a smile gracing his lips. He remembered the brave knight and the clever dragon, realizing how that initial story, though altered, had sparked his interest in heroism and problem-solving.

May, watching from afar, felt a warmth fill her heart. She knew that choosing the right stories for her son hadn't just filled his childhood with joy; it had helped him build a foundation for a kind and courageous life.

Tales with Timeless Lessons

In the vast tapestry of human experience, stories play a crucial role in shaping our understanding of the world. They are not just tales but guiding lights that offer timeless wisdom and insights. Let's dive into why stories with enduring lessons hold a special place in the hearts of storytellers and listeners alike.

1. Wisdom Weaved Into Narrative: These stories, like fables and parables or personal anecdotes, offer valuable insights that enrich with time, acting as a tapestry of wisdom.

2. Moral Compass: They serve as a moral compass (Greater Good Science Center, 2020), guiding us through life's journey with characters facing dilemmas and embracing virtues.

3. Navigating Morality: They help us understand the complexities of right and wrong, offering nuanced perspectives (Stanford Encyclopedia of Philosophy, 2023) and encouraging critical thinking.

4. Universal Truths: They resonate across cultures and time, sharing universal truths and fostering a sense of shared humanity.

5. Personal Growth: Ultimately, these stories allow for personal growth and reflection, offering a mirror to examine our choices and understand ourselves better.

6. Building Empathy: They build empathy by allowing us to see things from different perspectives, encouraging compassion and unity.

7. Inspiration and Resilience: These stories often feature characters who overcome challenges, inspiring us with resilience.

8. Teaching Values: For children, they are a fun way to learn important values (Harvard University, 2019), like kindness and honesty.

9. Bridging Generations: Shared stories become a way to bridge generations (StoryCorps, 2023), passing down wisdom and creating a legacy of values and connection.

10. Positive Change: The impact of stories with lessons goes beyond individual listeners, creating a ripple effect of positive change. Shared narratives shape our collective consciousness, influencing societal norms and values. In this way, storytelling becomes a catalyst for cultural evolution, inspiring communities to strive for compassion, justice, and progress.

In the heart of a bustling city lived Samantha, a single mother with a story etched into every wrinkle around her eyes. Her daughter, Jessica, a bright-eyed nine-year-old, loved nothing more than curling up beside her mother at night, listening to the tales Samantha weaved from her own past.

One evening, as the city lights twinkled outside their window, Samantha began, "There once was a little sparrow named Pip, who lived in a bustling nest atop a towering oak. Pip dreamed of soaring beyond the familiar branches, exploring the world beyond the city limits."

Jessica's eyes widened with anticipation. "Did he go, Mama?"

Samantha smiled. "Pip, unlike his siblings, was afraid of heights. He envied the other birds, their wings carrying them effortlessly across the sky. One day, a wise old owl named Hoot perched on the oak."

"What did Hoot say?" Jessica whispered, leaning closer.

"Hoot, with his gentle eyes, saw Pip's fear. He told him, 'The greatest journeys begin with a single step, even if it's just hopping off the branch.' Pip, inspired by Hoot's words, took a deep breath and leaped."

Jessica gasped. "Did he fall?"

Samantha chuckled. "Pip flapped his wings frantically, surprised by the wind beneath them. He wobbled, but slowly, he gained control. He looked back at the oak, then forward toward the vast blue sky. He realized that even the smallest bird could fly, as long as they had the courage to try."

As Samantha tucked Jessica into bed, she kissed her forehead. "Remember, honey, just like Pip, you too have the strength to overcome your fears and reach for your dreams."

Years passed, and the story of Pip became a bedtime staple. It wasn't just a story for Jessica anymore; it was a mantra, a reminder that courage could take flight in the most unexpected places. Jessica grew into a confident young woman, her heart filled with the same adventurous spirit she saw in Pip.

One day, Jessica received an acceptance letter to a prestigious university across the country. Fear threatened to hold her back, the distance seeming as vast as the sky Pip had once feared. But then, she remembered her mother's voice and Pip's story echoed in her mind.

Taking a deep breath, Jessica called her mother. "Mama," she said, her voice filled with a newfound determination, "I'm going to fly."

Samantha smiled, her heart swelling with pride. She knew, just like Pip, Jessica would find her own wind beneath her wings, her journey guided by the enduring lessons woven into the fabric of their shared story.

In the vast world of human stories, there are some that stand out like precious gems, shining with the wisdom they hold. These stories are timeless, crossing all boundaries of age, culture, and time and leaving a mark on all of us. When we dive into these tales, we're not just reading words on a page—we're taking a journey through our own hearts, where the lessons we learn will stay with us for a lifetime.

Chapter 8: Teaching Delayed Gratification

Delayed gratification is all about waiting for something bigger and better instead of taking something smaller and quicker right away. Imagine it like this: you would rather have the newest phone with the coolest features (bigger reward), even if it means waiting a few weeks to save up (waiting), instead of grabbing a cheap candy bar right now (smaller reward).

One of the most important lessons to teach your kids is the delay in gratification. A child's emotional resilience and long-term success are fundamentally based on developing patience, which is crucial in a society that frequently values quick fixes. Delayed gratification helps them develop self-control, patience, and the ability to plan for the future. These skills are vital not only for success in school but for developing strong relationships and showing patience in all aspects of life. Now let us take a closer look at what delayed gratification means and how parents may help their kids make this a life-changing experience.

Delayed gratification is the ability to resist the temptation of an immediate reward in favor of a more significant but deferred reward. Research like the Stanford Marshmallow Experiment (1972) highlights the power of delayed gratification. In this iconic study, psychologist Walter Mischel placed young children in a room with a tempting treat, often a marshmallow. The children were given a choice: eat the marshmallow immediately or wait for a short period to receive two marshmallows.

The Marshmallow Experiment linked a child's ability to wait for the second marshmallow with positive long-term outcomes like higher SAT scores, better physical health, and stronger social skills. Stories with lessons often mirror these benefits. They depict characters who achieve academic success through hard work and delayed gratification, maintain healthy habits by resisting temptations, and build strong relationships through patience and understanding.

Key Components of Delayed Gratification:

1. Time Perspective: Imagine you are at the store, and you see two treats: a small, yummy candy bar you can have right now and a giant, awesome ice cream sundae that you would need to save up for. This is a classic example of delayed gratification, a skill that helps us understand time perspective.

Time perspective simply means understanding that some things are more enjoyable if we wait for them. It is like planting a seed. You wait patiently, watering it every day, and eventually, you get a beautiful flower! The same goes for rewards. The small candy bar might satisfy you for a minute, but the giant sundae could be a special celebration with friends or family, making it a much more rewarding experience.

In the same way, this attribute can also be instilled in your child. Here is how:

Start small: Begin with short waiting periods. If your child wants a cookie before dinner, explain they can have one for dessert—a short wait for a sweeter reward.

Visualize the future: Use charts or calendars to track progress toward a desired toy. Seeing the wait time shrink builds excitement for the bigger reward.

Offer choices with a wait: Let them pick between a small snack now or a bigger treat after they finish their chores.

Make waiting fun: Create a "prize jar" where your child adds stickers, small toys, or beans for every day they wait for something big. This keeps them motivated and engaged.

2. Self-Control and Impulse Management: Fundamentally, the capacity to resist impulsive wants and cultivate self-control is essential for delayed gratification. Youngsters must be taught to ignore the instant appeal of a little reward in favor of a bigger payout down the road.

3. Goal Setting and Planning: Kids who are encouraged to make plans and set goals are instilled with a feeling of purpose. Through the process of breaking down more ambitious goals into smaller, more achievable milestones, a mindset that prioritizes long-term success over immediate gratification is fostered.

4. Emotional Regulation: Delayed gratification is closely linked to emotional regulation. Helping children identify and manage their emotions equips them with the tools to navigate the inevitable frustrations that may accompany waiting for a reward.

Make sure to acknowledge their patience! When they finally reach their goal, make a big deal about it. This reinforces the positive feelings associated with waiting. By teaching delayed gratification, you will equip your child with a valuable life skill. They will learn to make informed choices, prioritize long-term goals, and ultimately, experience the joy of waiting for something truly amazing. Read along to see how beneficial delayed gratification was for Daisy.

Being a tech-savvy mom, Daisy knew how much her son Ronald was obsessed with the latest VR headset. It was all he talked about, scrolling through endless videos highlighting its amazing games. He kept begging her to buy it, promising to do anything for it, even the extra chores that he utterly hated. His relentless persuasion put a thought in Daisy's mind – this was a perfect opportunity to teach him about delayed gratification.

"Ronald," she said, "that VR headset is awesome, but it's a big investment. How about we set a goal? If you save up half the money by doing extra chores and mowing the lawn, I will double your savings and buy it for you."

Ronald's face fell. Waiting? Ugh. But the thought of that powerful VR world spurred him on. Over the next few weeks, he hustled. He mowed lawns in the scorching sun, washed the car with meticulous detail, and even helped his neighbor bake cookies. Slowly, his piggy bank grew heavier.

Finally, the day arrived. Ronald beamed with pride as he presented his jar of coins to Daisy. Together, they reached their goal and bought the VR headset. The moment Ronald strapped it on, pure joy erupted. It was even better than he imagined because he had earned it through his effort and patience.

This experience taught Ronald a valuable lesson. Yes, instant gratification can be tempting, but waiting for something you truly desire and working toward it makes the reward all the sweeter. I bet this lesson won't just be a lesson for your child but for you too. Have patience and enjoy the fruits of your efforts!

Why does Delayed Gratification matter?

Delayed gratification is a very simple act of waiting, but it has surprising benefits that go way beyond treats!

Many studies have backed up the importance of self-control and delayed gratification. Besides the Marshmallow experiment, The Dunedin Multidisciplinary Health and Development Study also had remarkable findings. Children who exhibited greater self-control in their youth enjoyed better health, both physically and mentally, as adults. They also achieved greater success in their social and economic lives. This highlights the lasting impact of self-control, shaping well-being across various aspects of life.

Similarly, the University of Otago Longitudinal Study followed children from birth to adulthood. Their findings echoed the Dunedin study. Children with higher self-control and delayed gratification faced fewer health problems, were less likely to struggle with substance abuse, and encountered fewer legal issues throughout their lives. This reinforces the notion that self-control acts as a protective factor, leading to healthier and more fulfilling lives.

The lessons from these studies are clear: developing self-control and the ability to delay gratification are investments in our future. They pave the way for a healthier, happier, and more successful life. By teaching children these valuable skills, we empower them to navigate life's challenges with greater resilience and build a brighter future for themselves.

Here's how learning to wait can give your child a head start:

Academic Success: As stated in the studies above, kids who can wait tend to do better in school. They learn the discipline to focus on their studies, knowing the payoff of good grades comes later.

Higher Levels of Academic Motivation: Children who practice delayed gratification often display higher levels of academic motivation. They understand the connection between effort, perseverance, and academic success, fostering a positive attitude toward learning.

Emotional Resilience: Waiting teaches kids to cope with disappointment. When they learn rewards don't always come instantly, they develop resilience to bounce back from setbacks and healthily manage their emotions.

Enhanced Self-Control: Delayed gratification empowers children with enhanced self-control. They learn to manage impulses, resist temptations, and make decisions based on long-term considerations rather than immediate desires.

Elevated Emotional Intelligence: Delayed gratification contributes to heightened emotional intelligence. Children learn to understand and manage their emotions, conquer frustration, and approach challenges with a composed and thoughtful demeanor.

Financial Responsibility: Delayed gratification lays the groundwork for financial responsibility. Children who comprehend the value of saving and investing for future rewards are more likely to develop responsible financial habits in adulthood.

Stress Management: Patience contributes to effective stress management. Children who can wait for rewards are better equipped to handle challenging situations, exhibiting composure and resilience in the face of stressors.

Enhanced Problem-Solving Skills: Delayed gratification is closely tied to improved problem-solving skills. Children learn to approach challenges systematically, considering various options and anticipating potential outcomes before making decisions.

Reduced Impulsivity: The cultivation of delayed gratification reduces impulsivity. Children learn to resist impulsive actions, make thoughtful choices, and avoid hasty decisions that may have negative consequences.

Increased Empathy: Delayed gratification is associated with increased empathy. Children who are patient and considerate of others' needs develop a deeper understanding of different perspectives, enhancing their ability to empathize with the feelings and experiences of those around them.

Enhanced Cognitive Skills: The act of waiting for rewards stimulates cognitive development. Children engage in activities that require focus, concentration, and problem-solving, contributing to the enhancement of their overall cognitive skills.

Improved Decision-Making: Waiting makes kids think twice before acting. They learn to consider the consequences of their choices and weigh the long-term benefits over instant gratification. This helps them make thoughtful decisions that benefit them in the long run.

Building Healthy Habits: Patience is key to building good habits. Whether it's eating healthy, exercising, or practicing a skill, delayed gratification helps kids stick with it, paving the way for a healthy lifestyle.

Better Friendships: Waiting applies to relationships too! Kids who can wait their turn, compromise, and invest time in friendships build stronger and more meaningful connections with others.

Long-Term Goal Setting: The skill of delayed gratification encourages children to set and pursue long-term goals. They understand that meaningful achievements often require sustained effort over time, fostering a sense of purpose and direction.

Long-Lasting Satisfaction: Perhaps most importantly, delayed gratification teaches children the profound satisfaction derived from achieving meaningful goals over time. This intrinsic joy becomes a powerful motivator for continued growth and accomplishment throughout their lives.

To put it simply, the ability to postpone gratification is essential to the growth of a considerate and goal-oriented person. Parents and caregivers prepare children for a future full of success, emotional stability, and long-lasting fulfillment in life's accomplishments by teaching them this important skill.

Strategies for Teaching Delayed Gratification

Now you must be wondering how to teach your child this precious skill. It is very simple. Just follow through the steps given below:

1. Model Patience: Parents serve as primary role models. Demonstrating patience in daily life situations, from waiting in line to handling challenges, sets a powerful example for children to emulate.

2. Create Goal-Oriented Activities: Engage children in activities that require goal-setting and planning. This could range from a simple craft project to more complex endeavors like learning a musical instrument or participating in a sports team.

Engage children in the process of setting achievable goals. Whether it is completing a puzzle, learning a new skill, or finishing a book, establishing clear objectives encourages delayed gratification by promoting a sense of accomplishment upon completion.

3. Use Visual Aids: Utilize visual aids, such as countdown timers, to help children visualize the concept of time passing. This tangible representation reinforces the idea that rewards become more satisfying with patience. You can do this by creating a chart where children earn stickers for each day they complete their chores or tasks. After accumulating a certain number of stickers, they can receive a predetermined reward.

4. Celebrate Small Victories: Celebrate and give thanks for little victories along the way. Acknowledging progress—even in small steps—confirms the notion that achieving a goal involves many successful moments along the way.

5. Encourage Delayed Choices: Provide opportunities for children to make choices with delayed consequences. This might involve deciding between a quick treat and a more significant reward later, improving decision-making skills.

Integrate moments of waiting into daily routines. Whether it's waiting for a turn in a game, waiting for dinner to be served, or waiting for a preferred activity, these instances provide natural opportunities for children to practice patience.

6. Incorporate Games and Stories: Gamify learning by adding stories or games that emphasize the advantages of postponing gratification, such as the "Marshmallow Test," where children resist eating a treat for a specified period to earn a bigger reward. Children can relate to stories about characters who overcome obstacles by being patient. Board games, puzzles, and collaborative projects help children experience the satisfaction of seeing a task through to completion, emphasizing the value of patience.

7. Set Realistic Expectations: Help children understand that not all rewards require extended waiting. Setting realistic expectations about when to expect results encourages a balanced approach to delayed gratification.

8. Encourage Reflection: Prompt reflection on experiences that involve delayed gratification. Discuss what they learned, how they felt throughout the process, and the satisfaction derived from achieving a goal over time.

9. Read Books with Moral Lessons: Choose books that feature characters facing dilemmas and making decisions with long-term consequences. Discuss the stories with your child, emphasizing the importance of making choices that lead to positive outcomes in the end.

10. Teach Time Management Skills: Introduce basic time management skills to children. Use visual aids like timers or clocks to help them understand the concept of waiting and the reward that comes with completing a task or activity.

11. Engage in Long-Term Projects: Undertake projects that span over several days or weeks. This could be a gardening project, a science experiment, or a creative art endeavor. The anticipation of the final result encourages delayed gratification.

12. Create a "Waiting" Box: Establish a designated box filled with engaging activities for times when waiting is inevitable. This could include small puzzles, coloring books, or storybooks. The act of choosing an activity from the box teaches children to manage their impulses.

13. Teach Emotional Regulation: Help children identify and manage their emotions. Teaching them that it is okay to feel frustrated or impatient but providing healthy coping mechanisms, such as taking deep breaths or counting to ten, promotes emotional resilience.

14. Limit Instant Rewards: While occasional rewards are essential, limit instant gratification by encouraging the understanding that not every effort results in an immediate reward. Emphasize the joy of the journey and the sense of accomplishment when goals are achieved.

15. Involve Children in Decision-Making: Include children in age-appropriate decision-making processes. Discuss the potential consequences of different choices, encouraging them to consider the long-term impact of their decisions.

16. Praise Effort and Persistence: Shift the focus from outcomes to effort and persistence. Acknowledge and praise the hard work and dedication children put into tasks, emphasizing that true fulfillment often comes from the journey itself.

By implementing these techniques into regular interactions and activities, parents and other adults may contribute to the growth of delayed gratification abilities in children, giving them an important tool for overcoming obstacles and succeeding in the long run.

The Instant Gratification Epidemic

With the emergence of social media, human connection in the digital age has experienced a dramatic change. Although these platforms provide unprecedented levels of communication and information, they also introduce a daunting challenge: the youth's plague of instant gratification. The speed at which interactions occur online is fueling this phenomenon, which might have a significant impact on young people's relationships, mental health, and general well-being. Let me show you an example through Tabitha's story.

Tabitha scrolled through her phone, a familiar pang of envy twisting in her gut. Her friend Andria's post, a picture-perfect vacation in Bali, glowed on the screen. "Living my best life," the caption read, followed by a string of heart-eye emojis. Sending a like felt mandatory, but a niggling feeling lingered. Weren't they supposed to be saving for that camping trip this summer?

Later that evening, at dinner, Tabitha brought it up. "Isn't Andria struggling financially? How did she afford to go to Bali?"

Sam, Tabitha's dad, put down his fork. "Social media can be a highlight reel, Tab. People only show their best moments."

"But everyone seems to have these amazing lives," Tabitha grumbled. "It's not fair."

Sam smiled. "Life isn't a competition, honey. Real happiness comes from working toward goals, not chasing likes."

He reached over and showed her a faded photo. "See this? Your mom and I saved for months for this mountain trek. The view from the top was incredible, but the best part was the journey, the teamwork, the sense of accomplishment."

Tabitha looked at the photo, her parents beaming against a backdrop of snow-capped peaks. It wasn't Bali, but it held a quiet joy the filtered vacation photos lacked.

The next day, scrolling through Instagram, Tabitha noticed something new. Andria's "perfect" vacation photos seemed...empty. The posed smiles couldn't hide the underlying tension in her group. A caption about a fight with a friend stood out.

Suddenly, Tabitha realized the allure of instant gratification might be an illusion. True happiness comes from delayed gratification, the satisfaction of hard work, and genuine connection.

"Dad," she said, "Can we still go camping this summer?"

Sam smiled. "Absolutely. Let's start planning our adventure, one that might not get a million likes but will create memories that last a lifetime."

Tabitha grinned. Maybe this summer wouldn't be about Bali but about building a campfire, roasting marshmallows, and sharing stories under a sky full of stars. And that, she knew, was a story worth living.

So, the lesson we learn from Tabitha's story is that we don't need to envy things posted on social media. The real world moves gradually, bringing much grander prizes along with it. Here is a list of impacts on young minds from instant gratification:

1. The Pervasive Influence of Social Media: Social media platforms have become omnipresent in the lives of today's youth. Statistics calculated in 2021 reported that approximately 48.2% of the global population aged 13 to 17 years used social media.

Media platforms from Instagram to Snapchat thrive on immediacy—quick likes, instant comments, and the swift validation of online peers. Expectations in virtual and real-world interactions are shaped by the continuous flow of updates, which fosters an atmosphere where immediate feedback is accepted as the standard. This is truly hazardous for our children.

2. The Dopamine Dilemma: Social media thrives on instant dopamine hits. Likes, comments, and carefully curated feeds create a world of fleeting validation. This can warp their sense of accomplishment, making them crave those quick bursts of approval over the satisfaction of long-term goals. Studies by the University of California, Berkeley (2018) have shown a correlation between increased social media use and decreased focus and attention spans.

3. FOMO (Fear of Missing Out): The curated highlight reels on social media often cultivate a Fear of Missing Out (FOMO) among the youth. Seeing peers engaging in exciting activities, attending events, or forming new connections can intensify the desire for instant participation and gratification. The constant comparison can fuel a sense of inadequacy and the need to keep up with a perceived online standard.

4. Shallow Relationships and Communication: Quick, emoji-laden responses and brief comments have become the standard for online communication. While this brevity is convenient, it can lead to shallow interactions and hinder the development of deep, meaningful relationships. The emphasis on instant responses may undermine the value of thoughtful, nuanced communication.

5. Impatience and Unrealistic Expectations: The culture of instant gratification on social media can contribute to impatience and unrealistic expectations. Youth may develop a mindset that success, recognition, or accomplishments should materialize swiftly. This can create frustration when faced with the realities of gradual progress or delayed outcomes.

6. Health Implications: The instant gratification paradigm can take a toll on mental health. Continuous exposure to carefully curated online personas may lead to feelings of inadequacy, anxiety, or depression. The pressure to conform to online ideals can exacerbate existing mental health challenges and contribute to a sense of isolation. Excessive screen time, often attributed to social media use, has also been associated with sleep disturbances among youth. The blue light emitted by screens can interfere with the natural sleep-wake cycle.

7. Distorted Self-Perception: Social media platforms often showcase a polished version of reality, featuring filtered images and curated content. This curated portrayal can distort the self-perception of youth, promoting unrealistic beauty standards and lifestyle expectations. The quest for instant validation may lead to a perpetual cycle of comparison and dissatisfaction.

8. Short-Term Focus vs. Long-Term Goals: The culture of instant gratification may have an impact on young people's preference for immediate gratification over long-term objectives. Seeking immediate gratification could take precedence over the endurance and forbearance needed to attain significant goals or undergo personal development.

Instant gratification, while seemingly harmless in small doses, can harbor significant risks for children's development and well-being. Parents, educators, and caregivers must comprehend the possible drawbacks of instant gratification in this technologically advanced and fast-paced society. Let's examine the various ways that giving children too much quick satisfaction can harm them:

1. Undermining Patience and Perseverance: Excessive exposure to instant gratification can erode a child's capacity for patience and perseverance. The expectation of immediate rewards may diminish their willingness to invest time and effort in tasks that require sustained attention and commitment.

2. Impaired Decision-Making Skills: The habit of seeking instant rewards can impair a child's ability to make thoughtful and informed decisions. They may prioritize immediate pleasure without considering the long-term consequences, hindering the development of crucial decision-making skills.

3. Impact on Academic Performance: Instant gratification culture can negatively impact academic performance. Children accustomed to quick rewards may struggle with tasks that demand prolonged focus, such as studying for exams or completing assignments, potentially hindering their educational progress.

4. Shallow Interpersonal Connections: Shallow interpersonal ties may result from constant exposure to fast replies on social media and digital communication platforms. Youngsters may grow habituated to quick, surface-level interactions, which could hinder the emergence of deep connections.

5. Reduced Tolerance for Delay: The constant availability of immediate rewards can lead to a diminished tolerance for delayed gratification. Children may find it challenging to navigate situations where waiting is necessary, leading to frustration and potential behavioral issues.

6. Unrealistic Expectations: Instant gratification is common in many areas of life, and this can lead to inflated expectations. When faced with the reality of slow progress, children who grow up believing that success, happiness, or fulfillment should come at them instantly may become disappointed.

7. Potential for Addiction-Like Behavior: Seeking instant rewards can exhibit patterns akin to addiction. Children may develop habits of excessive screen time, seeking the next quick reward in the form of likes, comments, or digital entertainment, potentially leading to dependency issues.

8. Inhibition of Creativity and Exploration: Instant gratification may inhibit a child's exploration and creativity. The constant need for immediate feedback might discourage them from engaging in activities that involve experimentation, problem-solving, and the discovery of novel solutions.

9. Contributing to Attention Difficulties: The instant nature of digital stimuli can contribute to attention-related challenges. Children accustomed to rapidly changing content may struggle with sustained attention spans, impacting their ability to focus on tasks that require prolonged mental engagement.

A 2022 University of California, Los Angeles (UCLA) study found that frequent social media users exhibit a decreased ability to focus and stay engaged with complex tasks. This is likely due to the rapid-fire nature of social media content, which conditions our brains to expect constant novelty and immediate gratification.

Our capacity to perceive the complexity and depth of stories with timeless teachings may be hampered by this reduction in attention span. To properly understand the wisdom contained in these stories, prolonged concentration and thought are frequently necessary. We run the risk of losing the significance and deeper meaning of these stories when our focus is continually shifting from one post to another.

That being said, there is still hope. By practicing mindfulness in our social media usage and setting aside specific time for introspection and reading, we can develop the sustained attention span required to engage fully with stories that impart timeless teachings. By doing this, we can keep enjoying all of the numerous advantages that these stories provide, which include promoting empathy, personal development, and a better comprehension of the outside world.

10. Risk of Social Comparison and Low Self-Esteem: Social media is a prominent source of instant gratification and can expose children to the pressures of social comparison. Constantly comparing themselves to curated online personas may contribute to low self-esteem and a distorted self-image.

In today's digital age, social media presents a double-edged sword for our children. While it offers connection and information, it can also become a monster of instant gratification, chipping away at their patience and focus. As parents, our role is to be mindful mentors. We can't demonize social media entirely, but we can introduce it gradually and with boundaries. Encourage real-world interactions and hobbies that provide delayed gratification. Let them experience the joy of building something, mastering a skill, or nurturing a relationship—these rewards hold a deeper value than a fleeting online like.

Remember, we are their role models. Be mindful of your own social media habits. Engage in activities that demonstrate the value of delayed gratification—be it gardening, pursuing a creative project, or volunteering. Open communication is key. Talk to them about the curated nature of social media and the importance of self-worth beyond online validation. They can become responsible digital citizens who can navigate the complexities of social media without succumbing to its manipulative attraction if we help them develop better habits and a love of delayed gratification.

Tips for Parents to Help Kids Avoid Instant Gratification

Make them wait: Encourage activities that take time to finish, like building with Legos or planting a seed.

Limit screen time: Too much screen time can make kids want things right away. Set rules for how much screen time your child gets.

Watch social media: Keep an eye on what your child sees online. Social media can make kids feel like they need to have things right away.

Do real-life stuff together: Play games, cook a meal, or go for a walk. These activities help kids learn that some things are worth waiting for.

Be patient yourself: If you get upset when you have to wait, your child will too. Show them how to be patient by waiting calmly.

Help them set goals: Talk about things your child wants to achieve, like learning to ride a bike. Help them break down the goal into smaller steps.

Balance screen time with other activities: Make sure your child has time to play outside, read, and spend time with friends and family.

Talk about feelings: Let your child know it's okay to want things right away. Talk about how waiting can be hard, but it's worth it in the end.

Help them make choices: Let your child choose between two toys or activities. This helps them learn to think about what they want and make decisions.

Focus on the fun, not the reward: When your child does something good, give them credit for the effort as well as the result.

In short, delaying gratification is like having a superpower. It might seem tough at first, like waiting for two marshmallows instead of one, but the benefits last a lifetime. It can help your child control themself better, make smarter choices, and bounce back from difficulties easier. It sets your child up for academic achievement, financial responsibility, and strong emotional intelligence. And the benefits last well into adulthood, making them happier and healthier overall.

By letting your little one experience the satisfaction of delayed gratification, you are setting them up for success. You are equipping them with the tools to be strong, responsible, and happy adults. Wishing all the very best of luck in your parenting mission!

Chapter 9: Encouraging Persistence

Imagine parenting as a giant, epic quest. You are the hero with your little adventurer by your side, and every day brings a new challenge. Some days, it is a mountain of laundry that never seems to shrink. On other days, it is a tantrum that feels like it could power a small city. That is where persistence comes in, your secret weapon in this wild adventure.

Think of persistence as your ultimate superpower. It is like Captain America's shield that can deflect meltdowns and messy rooms. It is like Wonder Woman's bracelets, blocking the temptation to give up when bedtime battles rage for hours. It is not about being perfect, but about having the unwavering spirit to keep going, even when you trip over Legos (because you definitely will).

The best part? This superpower gets stronger the more you use it. Every time you patiently explain "no" for the hundredth time, your persistence muscle gets a workout. Every time you pick yourself up after a rough day and try again, your resilience grows. So, the next time you face a parenting challenge that feels like it has you cornered, remember: you've got this! Dust yourself off, channel your inner superhero, and keep moving forward. After all, the greatest adventures are rarely a straight shot to the finish line. It is the perseverance that makes the journey, and the little adventurer beside you makes it all the more rewarding.

Building Persistence

What do you think persistence in parenting means? Here are the three most important ways to incorporate the power of persistence as a parent:

Sticking to your guns: You have established a bedtime routine, and your child is fighting it? Be persistent. Explain the importance of sleeping calmly and consistently, even if it takes a few nights.

Following through: You said "no" to candy before dinner, and now the tears are flowing. Persistence doesn't mean giving in to every whim. It means sticking to your decisions with love and firmness.

Trying new approaches: Maybe your current method for potty training isn't working. Persistence means being patient, trying new strategies, and not giving up easily.

Remember, kids learn best through repetition. By being persistent, you are showing them the importance of following through, setting boundaries, and working toward goals. It doesn't mean you have to be rigid or unyielding. Persistence allows for flexibility and adjustment but within a framework of expectations.

The key is to be persistent with love and understanding. Explain your reasoning, offer choices when possible, and celebrate small victories. With consistent effort, your persistence will pave the way for a well-adjusted, responsible child.

A study published in the "Journal of Educational Psychology" by Duckworth et al. (2007) explored the concept of "grit"—a combination of passion and perseverance—and its role in predicting academic and professional success. The researchers found that individuals with higher levels of grit were more likely to achieve their long-term goals, surpassing those with greater talent but lower levels of persistence.

Moreover, longitudinal studies such as the "British Cohort Study" and the "National Child Development

Study" have provided compelling evidence linking persistence in childhood to a range of positive outcomes in adulthood. These studies, which followed participants over several decades, found that individuals who demonstrated perseverance and determination in childhood were more likely to attain higher levels of education, secure stable, well-paying employment, and experience greater overall life satisfaction in adulthood.

The results of this study have significant ramifications since they demonstrate how important persistence is in determining how people's lives turn out. Knowing the value of perseverance as parents enables us to help the next generation develop this crucial quality. We provide the foundation for future success by creating a positive atmosphere that promotes perseverance in the face of adversity, honors hard work and dedication, and instills a growth mentality that sees failures as chances for improvement.

The Growth Mindset Matters

The human brain is like a muscle. The more you use it and challenge it, the stronger it gets. A growth mindset is like believing you can make your brain stronger. As pioneered by psychologist Carol Dweck, a growth mindset is the belief that intelligence, abilities, and talents can be developed through dedication, effort, and learning. It not only cultivates resilience in the face of challenges but also nurtures a sense of agency and empowerment, laying the foundation for a lifelong journey of growth and achievement.

Strong evidence has been found connecting a growth mindset to increased resilience in the face of adversity and higher levels of accomplishment in both academic and non-academic domains through longitudinal studies like the "Project for Education Research That Scales (PERTS)". These studies highlight the transforming potential of attitudes and beliefs in influencing people's reactions to obstacles and failures.

There is a Japanese concept called Ikigai that focuses on finding your purpose in life and emphasizes continuous learning and growth. This aligns perfectly with the growth mindset. Here is why nurturing a growth mindset matters, backed by Ikigai:

- **Constant Improvement:** When you have a growth mindset, you see challenges as a way to learn and improve, like getting better at your weakest subject. You are not afraid to make mistakes because you know they help you grow.

Taking the concept of delayed gratification, we understand that every step in life requires effort and perseverance. The growth mindset teaches the concept of "not yet," which aligns with Ikigai's focus on continuous improvement. It means challenges are opportunities to learn and grow instead of limitations.

- **Never Stop Learning:** With a growth mindset, you believe you can always keep learning new things. This makes you more curious and excited to try new stuff!

- **Reach for the Stars:** You might not be the best at something right away, but that is okay! Ikigai suggests your purpose lies at the intersection of what you love, what you are good at, what the world needs, and what you can be paid for. Achieving mastery in any of these areas requires overcoming challenges. The growth mindset fosters this by viewing difficulties as stepping stones, not roadblocks.

Encouraging a growth mindset in kids requires us, as parents, teachers, and other caregivers, to provide a loving atmosphere that values hard work, perseverance, and learning from mistakes. The following are some methods to help kids develop a growth mindset:

1. Encourage Effort and Persistence: Praise your child for their hard work, dedication, and resilience in the face of challenges. Emphasize the process of learning and improvement rather than focusing solely on outcomes or innate abilities.

2. Provide Constructive Feedback: Offer specific and constructive feedback that focuses on the effort, strategies, and progress made by children rather than simply praising their intelligence or talents. Encourage them to view feedback as a valuable tool for growth and development.

3. Promote a "Yet" Mindset: Help your child to adopt a "yet" mindset, recognizing that they may not have mastered a skill or concept "yet," but with effort and perseverance, they can continue to improve over time.

4. Model a Growth Mindset: Lead by example by demonstrating a growth mindset in your attitudes and behaviors. Share stories of your challenges, setbacks, and moments of growth, highlighting the importance of perseverance and learning from failure.

5. Cultivate a Love of Learning: Integrate a curiosity and passion for learning by providing opportunities for exploration, discovery, and hands-on experiences. Encourage children to pursue their interests and passions, arming them with a lifelong love of learning.

Do you want to see how supporting your child in adopting a growth mindset will help in the future? Here is a heart-touching tale of a single father who helped his son shoot up to the skies from ground level.

The rhythmic glow of the computer monitor cast an alien light on Oliver's face as he furrowed his brows in concentration while navigating a fantastical online world. Piles of pending assignments lay abandoned on his study table, and yet Oliver was completely unbothered about them.

A sigh escaped Joseph's lips as he entered his son's room, the weight of his single-parent struggles settling on his shoulders. His only son, Oliver, had retreated further into the digital realm ever since those discouraging words from his teachers—a constant refrain about not being 'cut out' for academics or anything ambitious.

Joseph, a man who wore his share of life's bruises, knew that Oliver's demotivation wasn't apathy, but a shield built from repeated blows to his confidence. Tonight, he decided to try a different approach.

"Mind if I join you, buddy?" Joseph asked gently, his voice laced with a warmth that never failed to pierce Oliver's defenses.

Oliver glanced up with a flicker of surprise in his eyes before he mumbled a reluctant 'okay'. Joseph settled into the chair beside him, intending to connect instead of lecture. He started by reminiscing about his childhood dreams, of being an astronaut, a dream that fizzled out under the harsh realities of life. Oliver acted as though he was completely immersed in his game, but his ears listened intently to his father's words.

"But you know what, champ?" Joseph's voice softened, "Those dreams sparked a love for science in me. Even though I never reached the moon, that curiosity helped me land a pretty cool job as a mechanic, you know, fixing things and making them work."

Oliver found himself drawn into the conversation. A hesitant question peeked out from behind his usual silence, "But what if I'm just not good at anything, Dad?"

Joseph's heart ached for his son. Here was the crux of the issue, the self-doubt Oliver had been conditioned to believe.

"Hey," Joseph said, placing a hand on Oliver's shoulder, his touch grounding, "There's no 'good' or 'bad' at this stage, Oliver. It is about finding what excites you, what makes that spark ignite inside you. Remember that time you spent weeks tinkering with that old radio, trying to get it to work again?"

A shy smile tugged at Oliver's lips. He did remember the thrill of finally hearing static erupt from the speakers.

"That's it, champ!" Joseph's eyes shone with pride, not for some grand achievement, but for the flicker of rekindled passion in his son's eyes. "That's the fire you gotta chase. It won't always be easy, there will be setbacks, but that's okay. We will figure it out together, one step, one hurdle at a time. You got that 'yet' mindset, remember? You haven't mastered it yet, but with dedication, you can learn anything you set your mind to."

The seed of a new dream sprouted in Oliver's heart that night. With Joseph's support and a newfound belief in himself, he began to explore the world of technology with renewed zeal. The hours spent gaming transformed into coding classes, the frustration of failure replaced by the quiet satisfaction of progress. Years later, Oliver stood tall, not on the moon as Joseph once dreamt, but on a stage, accepting an award for his revolutionary tech start-up.

As the applause washed over him, Oliver's eyes met his father's in the crowd. A silent message passed between them, a culmination of countless late nights, pep talks, and strong faith. In Joseph's eyes, Oliver saw not just pride, but a deep gratitude, a word unspoken but understood. It was the gratitude for a father who didn't clip his son's wings but taught him to soar above the limitations others tried to impose.

Quite a heart-warming tale, right? I bet you wish the same for your little one. Then what are you waiting for? Go ahead and use your power of persistence and growth mindset to see your baby stand tall on that stage and look up to you as their inspiration.

The Art of Encouragement

Imagine your child struggling to make their science fair experiment. The figure keeps toppling over and they are about to give up in frustration. What do you do? This is where encouragement and celebration come in!

Encouragement is like magic fuel for kids. It gives them confidence and makes them want to keep trying. When you encourage your child, you are saying, "I believe in you, you can do it!"

Celebrating is like a high five for their effort. It shows them you are proud of what they have accomplished, no matter how small. It makes them feel good and want to do even better next time.

Here is the cool thing: science backs this up! It has been found that encouragement and celebration can help kids do better in school, sports, and pretty much everything they set their minds to.

A study published in the "Journal of Child and Family Studies" by Grolnick and Ryan (1989) found that parental encouragement and support were positively associated with children's self-esteem, motivation, and academic achievement. Similarly, Dweck and Leggett's (1988) research emphasized the value of rewarding effort and process above natural aptitude or results to help kids develop resilience and a growth mindset.

Here is how to encourage and celebrate your child like a pro:

1. Be Specific: Don't just say "Good job." Tell your child what you liked about what they did. For example, "I love how you kept trying different ways to build that tall Lego tower!"

2. Effort over Talent: Focus on how hard they tried, not just if they won or got the highest score. "You studied hard for that test, and that is what matters!"

3. Learn from Mistakes: Help your child see mistakes as a chance to get better. "That block tower fell, but let's see if we can build it even stronger next time!"

4. Big and Small Wins: Celebrate all their achievements, big or small. Finishing their homework? A reason to celebrate! Mastering a new bike trick? Party time!

5. High Fives All Around: Make your home a place where trying new things and learning are encouraged. Be their biggest cheerleader!

By encouraging and celebrating your child, you are helping them build persistence, which is a fancy way of saying they won't give up easily. They will learn to bounce back from setbacks and keep going for their dreams!

Efforts Over Results

As parents, we naturally want our children to succeed. We cheer their victories and beam with pride at their achievements. But what about the countless hours of practice, the stumbles and struggles that lead to those moments? Celebrating effort, not just results is a powerful way to nurture a growth mindset and resilient spirit in your child.

Imagine your child is struggling to learn a new piano piece. Their fingers fumble over the keys, frustration etched on their face. Instead of saying, "Why can't you get this right?" try, "Wow, that is a tricky part! I see you are practicing really hard. Keep at it, and you will get it soon." This acknowledges the effort and encourages them to persist.

Here is why celebrating effort is more important than just celebrating results:

1. Growth Mindset: Instead of saying, "You're a natural!" try, "Wow, I see you've been practicing that tricky part a lot. It sounds much smoother already!" This shows them that effort leads to improvement, not just talent.

2. Confidence Booster: When your child finishes a tough homework assignment, instead of just checking it, say, "Great job sticking with this! I know some of these problems were hard, but you figured them out." This builds their confidence to tackle future challenges.

3. Persistence Pays Off: Maybe your child loses a soccer game. Instead of focusing on the score, try, "You never gave up and kept trying to score that goal. That's what good sportsmanship is all about!" This teaches them that effort matters even when they don't win.

Steps to Celebrate Effort:

1. Notice the Effort: Pay attention to the hard work your child puts in, not just the outcome.

2. Be Specific: Instead of a generic "good job," point out the specific effort you see, "Wow, you practiced those scales really well today!"

3. Focus on Progress: Celebrate how far they've come, not just where they are. "You may not have won the race, but you ran your personal best!"

Being Patient as a Parent:

It's natural to want your child to succeed. But sometimes, success takes time. There will be times when your child won't achieve the results you hoped for. Here is where your patience comes in and your unwavering support becomes crucial.

Imagine you are planting a seed. You wouldn't expect a flower to bloom overnight, would you? Your child's growth and learning are similar. Celebrate their small victories along the way, and they will blossom into a confident and resilient person.

The worn biology textbook slammed shut as a gust of frustration ruffled Crystal's hair. Another C+ on her genetics quiz. Disappointment gnawed at her. Becoming a doctor had been her dream since childhood, a dream that her mother, Pearl, backed with firm support. Yet, despite hours spent hunched over textbooks, the As seemed perpetually out of reach.

Tears welled up in Crystal's eyes as she shuffled to her room with the crumpled quiz clutched in her hand. Moments later, Pearl's concerned voice cut through the silence, "Crystal, can I come in?"

Crystal mumbled a "Yes", already dreading the conversation. Her mother had a worried crease etching her brow as she saw the test grade. The tense silence stretched until Pearl finally spoke in a tight voice, "Is that how you will become a doctor, Crystal?"

The frustrated question shattered the dam within Crystal. Her tears began spilling freely. "I'm trying, Mom, I really am! But it's just so hard."

Pearl's own voice cracked a flicker of vulnerability in her eyes. "I know, honey, I know it is. But..." she trailed off, then took a deep breath. "There's something I haven't told you."

Crystal looked up in surprise. She had expected more lecturing, but her mother sounded a bit tired. Although, that made her feel worse about herself, she felt like there was more to the story.

Pearl sat beside her on the bed, her hand seeking Crystal's. "When I was younger," she began, "I had dreams too. Big dreams." She hesitated, then continued, "But life had other plans. Responsibilities piled up, and I never got the chance to chase them."

A new understanding dawned on Crystal. Maybe her mother's push wasn't just about her, but about a second chance at a dream, a chance Crystal was supposed to fulfill. The weight of that expectation, however, was crushing.

"I see your frustration, Crystal," Pearl continued in a softer tone. "But listen to me. This journey of becoming a doctor is a marathon, not a sprint. There will be setbacks and times you stumble. But what matters is that you keep going."

Pearl squeezed Crystal's hand. "There is a new approach we can try. It is called a growth mindset. It is about focusing on the effort you put in, on learning and improving, not just the end result."

Crystal's mind whirred. Maybe it wasn't all about getting straight As. Maybe the countless hours spent studying and the determination to understand complex medical concepts, those things mattered too.

"You won't win every battle, Crystal," Pearl admitted, "and yes, even moms lose their temper sometimes. But I want you to remember this: Your effort always matters. And sometimes, even if you give your all, things won't go according to plan. That's okay because that is life. But if you really want to achieve your dreams you should never give up no matter what."

Tears welled up in Crystal's eyes, but this time they weren't disappointed tears. Instead, they were more about the hours she had spent hating herself for being incompetent. It wasn't just about becoming a doctor anymore. It was about the journey, the resilience, the unwavering spirit her mother had instilled in her.

The next morning, Crystal woke up with a renewed sense of purpose. The biology textbook no longer seemed daunting. It was a challenge, yes, but one she was ready to face, one step, one lesson at a time. The path to becoming a doctor might have unexpected turns, but Crystal knew one thing for sure: effort mattered more than the final grade.

Remember as a parent, you are not just raising an athlete, artist, or scholar; you are raising a human being. Developing a strong work ethic, resilience, and the ability to learn from mistakes are far more valuable than any single trophy or grade.

Parenting is a demanding yet rewarding journey. By celebrating the effort, you become your child's biggest cheerleader, instilling in them the confidence and determination to keep striving because that is what truly makes success a meaningful journey. That's why your job is so important! It is not about pushing for immediate results but nurturing a love of learning and the perseverance to keep trying. It takes time and patience, but the rewards are a child who is self-motivated, resourceful, and ready to take on the world!

Chapter 10: The Toddler Tantrum Toolbox

Parenthood is a beautiful and occasionally ear-splitting journey filled with more love than a Hallmark movie marathon and more meltdowns than a toddler-fueled ice cream social. Let us face it, tantrums are a guaranteed part of the parenting package, right up there with sleepless nights and enough "Mommy, watch this!" moments to make you question your sanity.

This chapter is dedicated to all the brave parents who have ever navigated the treacherous terrain of Tantrum Territory. Remember that time when your perfectly angelic child launched into a full-blown opera in the cereal aisle because you dared suggest anything other than Fruit Loops? Or the epic meltdown in the checkout line because of reasons beyond your understanding? Well, you are not alone!

Join me on a trip through the fascinating world of toddler emotions. Explore the "whys" behind the tantrums and equip yourself with a survival kit full of strategies to navigate these meltdowns with grace (and maybe a little chocolate for celebration). So, grab your noise-canceling headphones, and read on to figure out the solution to all the problems in your life.

Why Do Kids Have Tantrums?

Do you agree that this question has haunted a parent a million times in life? Do you recognize that feeling when you are out shopping, at the park, or having a quiet dinner at home, and suddenly your child erupts in a full-blown tantrum? It can leave you flustered and wondering what on earth just happened. Anyways, you can't expect your baby to always be a little angel. Face the bitter truth: your kids won't listen to you all the time.

In order to manage your kid's tantrums, the first thing you have to do is learn to understand them. This is not always as simple as it sounds, since tantrums are generated by a lot of different emotions: fear, frustration, anger, sensory overload, or even the lack of attention. Moreover, children are in the stage of developing their cognitive and language skills, which means they may not always understand or process instructions as quickly or effectively as adults. They also have shorter attention spans and may become easily distracted by their surroundings, making it challenging for them to focus on what you are saying.

Tantrums are normal, especially in young children. It is useful to think of a tantrum as a reaction to a situation that a child can't handle in a more mature manner. They are a medium to communicate their frustrations and big emotions since they don't quite have the words for it yet. So, instead, when the child feels overwhelmed by emotions, he releases his feelings by crying, yelling, stomping his feet, punching the wall, or even if worse comes to worse, hitting a parent. If such a response gets him what he wants, the child learns to rely on that behavior and make it a conditioned response.

"Even if it only works five out of ten times that they tantrum, that intermittent reinforcement makes it a very solid learned behavior," Dr. Lopes explained. "So they are going to continue that behavior in order to get what they want."

That doesn't mean that tantrums are deliberate or even voluntary. But it does mean that they are a learned response. So, the goal with a child prone to tantrums is to help him *unlearn* this response, and learn more mature ways to handle a problem situation, like compromising or complying with parental expectations in exchange for some positive reward.

Understanding what triggers your child's tantrums is the first step in helping them manage their outbursts. Mental health professionals call this process a "functional assessment." It involves carefully examining real-life situations that seem to lead to tantrums. This assessment looks at what happens immediately before, during, and after the tantrum to identify factors that might be contributing to the behavior and potentially causing future breakdowns.

Sometimes, a closer look at these patterns can reveal underlying issues that need to be addressed. These issues could range from a past traumatic experience or abuse to social anxiety, ADHD, or a learning disability. When children experience tantrums or meltdowns beyond the age where they are typically expected, it is often a sign of emotional distress that they are struggling to manage on their own. This struggle can lead to breakdowns at moments that require self-control, a skill set that is still developing in young children. Transitions from enjoyable activities to more challenging tasks can be particularly difficult for them to handle, triggering outbursts.

Vasco Lopes, PsyD, a clinical psychologist said, "A majority of kids who have frequent meltdowns do it in very predictable, circumscribed situations: when it's homework time, bedtime, time to stop playing. The trigger is usually being asked to do something that is aversive to them or to stop doing something that is fun for them. Especially for children who have ADHD, something that is not stimulating and requires them to control their physical activity, like a long car ride or a religious service or visiting elderly relatives, is a common trigger for meltdowns." This gist is that you have to decipher the triggers for their behaviors.

The objectives of the functional assessment are to see if some tantrum triggers might be eliminated or changed to make them less problematic for the child. You can change the way you handle a situation to defuse it. This could mean restructuring the activities to reduce the likelihood of a tantrum.

"Anticipating those triggers, and modifying them so that it's easier for the child to engage in that activity is really important," says Dr. Lopes. "For example, if homework is really difficult for a child because she has underlying attention, organization, or learning issues, she might have outbursts right before she's supposed to start her homework. So, we say to parents, 'How can we make doing homework more palatable for her?' We can give her frequent breaks, support her in areas she has particular difficulty with, organize her work and break intimidating tasks into smaller chunks."

Here are some possible reasons why your little one might be throwing a tantrum:

- **They are tired, hungry, or uncomfortable.** These basic needs are a big deal for little people, and when they're not met, it can lead to a meltdown.

- **They don't get what they want.** Maybe you said no to a toy, or they can't quite reach that cookie jar. As toddlers try to seek their independence, they often bump against the boundaries we set. This can lead to power struggles as a child thinks "I can do it myself" or "Give me what I want!" When kids discover that they can't have everything they want, they get frustrated which leads to outbursts.

- **They are overwhelmed by their emotions.** Loud noises, crowded places, or even just a change in routine can be overwhelming for young children, leading to a tantrum.

- **They are seeking attention.** Sometimes, even negative attention is better than no attention at all. Your little one might have figured out that acting out is the quickest way to get your attention.

It is important to keep in mind that avoiding a tantrum does not mean "giving in" to your child, it means separating unwanted tantrum responses from issues such as listening to a parent's requests. Secondly, reducing the possibility of a tantrum takes away the opportunity for reinforcement of that response. Avoiding tantrums teaches children how to handle needs, wants, and disappointments in a more responsible manner, which in turn reinforces the right answers. Fewer tantrums today translate into fewer tantrums later on in life.

Identifying the Signs

Recognizing the patterns of frustration in children helps parents to effectively support their emotional well-being and address their needs. While children may express frustration in countless ways depending on their age, temperament, and personality, there are some common signs that parents can look out for:

1. Verbal Expressions: Younger children may express frustration through verbal cues, such as crying, whining, or saying phrases like "I can't do it" or "It is too hard." Older children may use words to express their frustration, such as complaining, expressing dissatisfaction, or using negative language.

2. Physical Symptoms: Frustration can also manifest through physical symptoms, such as stomping feet, clenched fists, tense muscles, or facial expressions of anger or distress. Some children may exhibit behaviors like hitting, biting, or throwing objects out of frustration. Even constant fidgeting, tapping feet, or being unusually silent are signs that you can look out for.

3. Withdrawal or Avoidance: In some cases, children may withdraw or avoid situations that trigger feelings of frustration. They may become quiet, retreat to their room, or disengage from activities or interactions with others.

4. Changes in Behavior: Frustration can also lead to changes in behavior, such as increased irritability, moodiness, or defiance. Children may become more argumentative, resistant to authority, or exhibit oppositional behavior as a way of expressing their frustration.

5. Difficulty Concentrating: Children experiencing frustration may have difficulty concentrating or staying focused on tasks. They may become easily distracted, lose interest in activities, or struggle to complete tasks that they previously enjoyed.

Understanding your child's frustration is the first step to helping them manage it. By acknowledging their feelings and responding with patience and empathy, you create a safe space for them to express themselves. This gives them the message that it is okay to feel frustrated and upset. Imagine yourself in their shoes—frustration is a normal part of life, especially for young children.

The good news is that you can help your child develop healthy coping mechanisms. By offering support and guidance, you'll equip them with the tools they need to confront tough emotions and find solutions. Remember, a little frustration today can lead to greater resilience and emotional intelligence tomorrow.

How Can You Avoid Tantrums?

You are definitely familiar with the phrase "Prevention is better than cure." Therefore, your priority should be to try to prevent tantrums from happening in the first place. Here are some methods that may help:

Shower with positive attention. Get in the habit of paying attention when your child is being good. Reward your little one with praise and attention for positive behaviors. Be specific about praising behaviors you want to see happen more often, such as, "I like the way you said please and waited for your treat" or "Thank you for sharing your toys with your sister."

Give control over little things. Offer minor choices such as "Do you want a banana shake or strawberry shake?" or "Do you want to brush your teeth before or after taking a bath?" This way, you aren't asking "Do you want to brush your teeth now?"—which of course will be answered "No."

Allow control when it doesn't matter. Instead of struggling over an outfit your child puts on that doesn't match, maybe consider whether this may be an opportunity to allow self-expression and independence and if it really makes a difference given the day's schedule.

Stop temptations. See if you want to make your struggles easier, don't tempt your kid. This means keeping off-limits objects out of sight and out of reach. Obviously, this isn't always possible, especially outside of the home where the environment can't be controlled, but you have to make sure to try your best.

Distract your child. Try offering something else in place of what they cannot have. Start a new activity to replace the frustrating or forbidden one. For example, if your child is jumping on the couch, ask them to come help you "cook" by offering your guidance. Then you can praise them for helping or following directions, rather than having them start a tantrum or refuse to get down. Or simply change the environment. Take your toddler outside or move to a different room.

Teach new skills and succeed. Help kids learn to do things on their own. Praise them to help them feel confident in what they can do. Also, try to start with something simple before moving on to more challenging tasks.

Consider your child's request carefully. Is it something that is impossible for you to agree to? Or maybe you could actually complete it. Make a wise choice when choosing your battles. There is nothing wrong with changing your mind if you originally said no. But find a way to allow the desired treat as a reward for good behavior.

Know your kid's limits. If you know your toddler is tired, it is not the best time to go grocery shopping or try to squeeze in one more errand. Hungry kids are more likely to demand food in the store than children who have just had a meal.

Reacting to Tantrums

Most parents react in various ways when faced with their child's tantrums. Common reactions often include anger, impatience, or even resorting to yelling or punishment. While these reactions may be understandable given the stress and exhaustion of parenting, they can have adverse effects on both the parent-child relationship and the child's emotional development.

Reacting with anger or impatience to a child's frustration can escalate the situation and make it more challenging to resolve. When a parent responds with anger or harshness, it can heighten the child's emotional distress, leading to increased tantrum intensity or feelings of shame and inadequacy. This can create a cycle of negative behavior and communication patterns, eroding trust and undermining the bond between the parent and child.

As a parent, you need to model the kind of behaviors that you want your child to learn. "Parents should take time outs, too," notes Dr. Dickstein. When you get really angry you need to just take yourself out of the situation. You can't solve problems when you are upset—your IQ drops about 30 percent when you are angry."

It is important for parents to approach these situations with patience, empathy, and understanding. By validating children's feelings, and offering support and guidance, parents can help children learn healthy ways of managing their emotions and build stronger, more trusting relationships with their children. Consider making a "chill out" or "calm down" spot in your home. Use a soft cushion and provide books, a stuffed animal, some soft music, and other calming activities in a place where others won't disturb the child. Encourage your child to go to the spot when angry or upset—not as a punishment, but as a choice and an opportunity to learn to calm down and control frustration.

Dr. Lopes gives clear instructions regarding this. He explained that instead of 'You need to behave today,' parents should say 'You need to be seated during mealtime, with your hands to yourself, and saying only positive words.' Those are very observable, concrete things that the child knows what is expected and that the parent can reinforce with praise and rewards. Also, remember to be consistent with your approach. Don't give in to the same requests sometimes and then expect different results.

Both you and your child need to build what Dr. Dickstein calls a toolkit for self-soothing, things you can do to calm down, like breathing slowly to relax, because you can't be calm and angry at the same time. There are lots of techniques, he adds, but "The nice thing about breathing is that it is always available to you."

Your reactions to a tantrum play a big role in whether it happens again. When your child throws a tantrum, it is important to resist giving them what they want to stop the outburst. This might seem counterintuitive, but giving in teaches them that tantrums are an effective way to get things.

Here are some key points and therapy approaches mentioned:

Ignore the Tantrum: The most effective strategy for non-dangerous outbursts might be to ignore the behavior. This means withdrawing all attention, both positive and negative. Don't yell, argue, or try to reason with your child.

Why Ignoring Works: Even negative attention can be rewarding to a child throwing a tantrum. Ignoring the behavior shows them it won't get them what they want. This can be difficult, but stay calm and wait for the tantrum to pass.

Collaborative & Proactive Solutions (CPS) by Ross Greene: This approach focuses on identifying and addressing the underlying reasons behind your child's tantrums. It emphasizes collaborative problem-solving between parent and child. In order to add this to your routine, follow these guidelines:

- **Shift your perspective:** View challenging behavior as a sign your child is struggling, not being disobedient.

- **Identify lagging skills:** What skills might your child be lacking that are leading to the behavior? Is it frustration management, problem-solving, or difficulty expressing emotions?

- **Collaborate with your child:** Work together to brainstorm solutions that address the lagging skill and prevent the challenging behavior.

- **Focus on proactive solutions:** Instead of just reacting to bad behavior, create proactive plans to address potential difficulties.

Parent-Child Interaction Therapy (PCIT) & Parent Management Training (PMT): These therapy programs teach parents specific skills and strategies to improve communication and interactions with their children. It involves techniques to de-escalate situations, set clear expectations, provide positive reinforcement, and use effective consequences. Here is how you can do this:

- **Focus on positive interactions:** Spend quality time playing and connecting with your child.

- **Use clear and concise commands:** Be specific about your expectations, and avoid lengthy explanations.

- **Offer positive reinforcement:** Praise good behavior and effort.

- **Implement consistent consequences:** Follow through with pre-determined consequences for misbehavior.

Keeping your calm and clear about behavioral expectations is important because it helps you communicate more effectively with your child. Remind yourself that your job is to help your child learn to be calm. For this, you need to be calm yourself. Here are some practical strategies for parents to stay calm when faced with tantrums and how to react during them:

1. Take a Deep Breath: When you feel yourself getting frustrated or overwhelmed, take a moment to pause and take a deep breath. Deep breathing can help activate the body's relaxation response and calm your nervous system, allowing you to approach the situation with a clearer mind.

2. Practice Mindfulness: Mindfulness techniques, such as meditation or mindful breathing, can help you stay present and grounded in the moment. By focusing on your breath or sensations in your body, you can reduce stress and anxiety and cultivate a sense of inner peace and calm.

3. Give Yourself a Timeout: If you feel yourself becoming too overwhelmed or upset, it is okay to step away from the situation temporarily. Give yourself a timeout by taking a short walk, stepping into another room, or engaging in a calming activity like listening to music or practicing yoga.

Be realistic about what you can accomplish and how much you can handle in a given day. Don't put too much pressure on yourself to be a perfect parent or have everything under control. Give yourself permission to prioritize self-care and take breaks when needed.

4. Use Positive Self-Talk: Replace negative or self-critical thoughts with positive affirmations and self-talk. Remind yourself that you are doing the best you can and that it is okay to make mistakes. Be kind and compassionate to yourself, just as you would to your child.

5. Seek Support: Don't hesitate to reach out to a partner, family member, or friend for support when you are feeling overwhelmed. Sometimes, talking to someone who can offer perspective or a listening ear can help you gain clarity and perspective on the situation.

6. Focus on Solutions: Instead of dwelling on the problem or what went wrong, focus on finding solutions and moving forward. Identify what you can control in the situation and take proactive steps to address it. Remember that every challenge is an opportunity for growth and learning.

7. Practice Empathy: Try to see the situation from your child's perspective and empathize with their feelings. Understand that they may be acting out of frustration, fear, or confusion, and respond with empathy and compassion rather than anger or judgment.

8. Validate Feelings: Acknowledge your child's feelings and let them know that it is okay to feel upset or frustrated. Use empathetic statements such as, "I understand that you are feeling angry right now," or "It is okay to be upset, but we need to find a solution together."

9. Set Limits: While it is essential to validate your child's feelings, it is also important to set limits on behavior. Let your child know what behavior is unacceptable and establish clear consequences for tantrums, such as a time-out or loss of privileges.

10. Redirect Attention: Sometimes, distracting or redirecting your child's attention can help defuse a tantrum. Offer them a toy, book, or activity to focus on instead of dwelling on their frustration.

11. Use Positive Reinforcement: Praise your child for using positive coping strategies or for calming down after a tantrum. Positive reinforcement can help reinforce desired behaviors and encourage your child to use healthier ways of expressing their emotions in the future.

12. Teach Coping Skills: Help your child develop coping skills to manage their emotions more effectively. Encourage deep breathing exercises, counting to ten, or using a calm-down corner where they can go to take a break and regroup when feeling overwhelmed.

13. Model Healthy Coping: Children often learn by example, so it's essential to model healthy coping strategies in your own behavior. Demonstrate how to manage frustration calmly and positively, even when faced with challenges or setbacks.

14. Reflect and Learn: After the situation has passed, take some time to reflect on what happened and what you can learn from it. Consider what triggered your frustration and how you can better respond in similar situations in the future. Every experience is an opportunity for growth and self-improvement.

Remember that every child is unique, and what works for one child may not work for another. It may take time and patience to find the strategies that are most effective for managing your child's frustration and tantrums. By approaching these situations with empathy, understanding, and consistency, you can help your child learn to face their emotions in a healthy and constructive way.

What Should You Do After a Tantrum?

Praise your child for regaining control—for example, "I like how you calmed down." Kids may be especially vulnerable after a tantrum when they know they have been disobedient. When your child is calm, give him a hug and reassure him that he is loved, no matter what. If your child is old enough to discuss the problem, help them come up with some other ways they might have expressed their frustration.

Ensure your kids get adequate rest. Children who don't get enough sleep can behave in extreme ways and become hyper and irritable. Sleeping enough is one way to significantly lower tantrums. Find out how much sleep your child needs, given their age. Although every child is different, most children's sleep needs fall within a specific range of hours depending on their age.

In case your child still keeps showing aggressive behaviors after using all these strategies, try consulting a doctor for advice. If you often feel angry or out of control when responding to tantrums, end up giving in when your child acts out, and have face extreme consequences from the behaviors, please don't hesitate to get a professional's help. I hope everything works out for you!

Thirteen-year-old Kevin slammed the front door, and the sound echoed through the empty house. Monica, his mother, flinched in surprise as she looked up from her paperwork. This wasn't the first time Kevin had come home in a rage, but lately, it seemed to be happening more and more. Tonight, a fresh scrape marred his knuckles.

"Kevin? Honey, what happened?" Monica called out, concern lacing her voice.

Kevin stomped into his room and slammed the door shut with another resounding thud. Monica sighed, the worry tightening in her chest. She knew things were tough for Kevin at school. He had confided in her about the taunts and snickers—the constant feeling of being different. But lately, he had withdrawn, retreating into a silent shell at home. Monica, swamped with work and her own anxieties, hadn't noticed the telltale signs—the clenched fists and mumbled frustrations.

Tonight, she decided things had to change. Taking a deep breath, she knocked gently on Kevin's door. "Kevin, can I come in?"

Silence. Monica hesitated, then pushed the door open a sliver. Kevin was sprawled on his bed with his back to her, a red mark blooming on his arm. Panic surged through her.

"Kevin!" she cried, rushing to his side. He flinched away, his voice raw.

"Leave me alone!"

Monica held back, her voice gentling. "Honey, let me see that."

Kevin reluctantly showed her his arm. Tears welled in her eyes. "Why, Kevin? Why are you hurting yourself?"

He looked away, shame flickering across his face. The words tumbled out in a torrent. The relentless teasing, the feeling of isolation, the constant pressure to fit in. He spoke of his loneliness and the feeling of being invisible even at home. Monica listened, her heart aching with each word.

When he finished, a heavy silence settled between them. Monica sat beside him in silence. She knew sometimes, the most powerful words were no words at all. It was a lesson in patience, a realization that sometimes, a listening ear is all a child needs.

Finally, she spoke, her voice soft. "Kevin, I'm so sorry. I haven't been the mom you needed lately. Work has been overwhelming, but that is no excuse." She squeezed his hand gently. "You are not alone, okay? I'm here for you, always."

Kevin looked at her, a flicker of hope in his eyes. They talked for a long time that night, and Monica truly listened, offering support and understanding. She promised to help him through the challenges at school and to advocate for him. They made a plan to spend more time together, just the two of them.

It wasn't a magic fix. There were still rough days and moments of frustration. But the tantrums lessened, replaced by open communication. Kevin started confiding in Monica again, finding strength in her love and support. Monica, in turn, learned a valuable lesson about patience—the importance of being present for her son, not just physically but emotionally. She discovered that sometimes, the greatest strength lies in simply listening, in letting a child know they are seen, heard, and loved unconditionally. And in that quiet understanding, they found a way to navigate the storms of adolescence together. I hope this beautiful tale also inspires you to be a better parent because you have to fulfill your responsibility for the dear little angels you brought into this world.

By understanding your own and your child's frustrations, you can create a more positive household. This, in turn, helps children develop healthy ways to manage their emotions and bounce back from challenges. The ultimate goal is finally a stronger parent-child relationship built on empathy and support. Imagine a home where everyone feels heard and understood—that is the power of this approach. With a little effort and a commitment to empathy, families can build a foundation of peace and connection that benefits everyone, now and in the future.

Remember, building strong family bonds takes time and effort. Now, it is on you to create a sense of harmony, peace, and connection by cooperating and putting patience first, which will ultimately benefit everyone in the long run.

Remember, tantrums usually aren't cause for concern and generally stop on their own as kids mature and gain self-control. They learn to cooperate, communicate, and cope with frustration. Less frustration and more control will mean fewer tantrums—and happier parents. It is best to try and be patient for that time to come. Best of luck!

Chapter 11: Setting Realistic Expectations

Setting realistic expectations for both you and your children is like finding the sweet spot between challenging them to grow and recognizing their current capabilities. Imagine expecting a toddler to sit through a two-hour movie without fidgeting or a teenager to never argue with parental rules. Sounds like a script for a comedy movie, right? These scenarios remind us of the humorous side of parenting, illustrating how unrealistic expectations can set the stage for unnecessary frustration on both sides.

Unrealistic expectations are like setting the GPS for a destination without considering road closures or traffic; it leads to unnecessary delays and, sometimes, giving up on reaching the destination altogether. In parenting, unrealistic expectations can similarly detour the developmental journey of a child and strain the parent-child relationship. It can manifest in pushing a child too hard to excel in every area, expecting perfection in behavior at all times, or comparing siblings. Each of this may lead to a mix of frustration, disappointment, and even resentment.

Remember the scene from the movie *Finding Nemo* where Marlin, the overly protective clownfish father, has to learn to trust his son's capabilities and loosen his grip? It's a heartwarming reminder that children, much like Nemo, often exceed our expectations when given trust and freedom to explore. Contrary to that is the classic tale of the overambitious stage parent, illustrated with humor and exaggeration in *Little Miss Sunshine*. The movie not only makes us laugh but also poignantly highlights the absurdity and consequences of projecting our unrealized dreams or unreasonable demands onto our children.

So, this chapter is not about lowering your expectations to the point of non-existence but about aligning them with the reality of your child's developmental stage, individual temperament, and unique abilities. It's about adjusting the sails as you navigate the parenting, knowing when to be firm and when to let go, and understanding that every child's map to success is uniquely theirs.

In this chapter we will explore how to set, communicate, and adjust expectations in ways that support your child's growth into a confident and resilient individual. We will share strategies and insights to keep things relatable and light-hearted. Because, at the end of the day, parenting is not about crafting the perfect child but about guiding, supporting, and celebrating the unique individual your child is becoming.

Infancy: The Foundation

During infancy stage, the first two years of your baby, your baby's brain is like a sponge, absorbing everything. It's a time of rapid physical growth, cognitive development, and emotional attachment. Remember the scene in *Look Who's Talking* when Mikey navigates his new world? Though exaggerated, the movie amusingly captures the infant's perspective—discovering their environment, recognizing voices, and forming bonds. This stage is about providing a nurturing and stimulating environment. You will marvel at their first smile, the first time they recognize you, and their first attempts at words. It's a period filled with 'firsts', each a building block for future stages.

Toddlerhood: The Exploration

Ages two to four are marked by a surge in independence, language development, and motor skills. Toddlers are notorious for their boundless energy and curiosity. They are like the animated character Curious George, whose adventures mirror a toddler's daily life—full of exploration, learning, and, yes, occasional mischief. This is the stage where 'why' is a favorite word of your child, and every drawer or cupboard is a mystery to solve. Emotionally, toddlers start asserting their independence, which can lead to memorable (if challenging) tantrums. It's a time for patience and setting boundaries, teaching them the beginnings of empathy and cooperation through play and interaction.

Preschool: The Socialization

As children enter the preschool stage, ages four to six, their world expands significantly. They become more engaged in social interactions and begin to form real friendships. Think of Woody and Buzz from *Toy Story*—initial rivals who become inseparable friends through shared experiences. Preschoolers learn the value of friendship, sharing, and teamwork. Their cognitive abilities allow for more complex play and problem-solving, setting the stage for formal learning. Emotional development takes a front seat as they experience a wider range of emotions and begin to understand the feelings of others.

School Age: The Learner

The school-age years, from six to twelve, bring about a transformation in cognitive abilities. Children become capable of logical thought processes, and their academic journey begins in earnest. Remember Hermione Granger from the *Harry Potter* series? Her insatiable curiosity and skill at picking up new spells perfectly capture the cognitive growth of a school-age youngster. This period is crucial for developing a sense of competence and self-esteem as they tackle new challenges. Emotionally, children become more adept at understanding complex emotions and empathy, though peer influence becomes a significant factor in their development.

Adolescence: The Identity Seeker

Adolescence is a tumultuous time, characterized by a search for identity and independence. Think of Simba in *The Lion King*, embarking on a journey of self-discovery, facing challenges, and eventually finding his place in the circle of life. Adolescents question authority, seek autonomy, and develop deeper relationships outside the family. Cognitive abilities are close to adult levels, allowing for abstract thought and moral reasoning. Emotionally, it's a rollercoaster, with the quest for identity often leading to mood swings and conflicts, but ultimately toward a coherent sense of self.

Bringing It All Together

Understanding these developmental stages helps us as parents to set realistic expectations, provide appropriate support, and enjoy the unique journey of each child. It's important to remember that each child is unique and may not fit neatly into these stages or follow the exact timeline. The anecdotes and examples from movies, while entertaining, remind us of the universal nature of growing up, the challenges faced at each stage, and the triumphs that come with overcoming them.

The Impact of Expectations on Children

When we think about the role of a parent, it often comes wrapped in the unspoken job description of being a guide, a teacher, and sometimes, a bit of a project manager for our children's lives. The blueprint we follow often comes from our expectations, a set of beliefs about what our children should achieve and how they should behave. But here's where it gets tricky: our expectations, much like a double-edged sword, can either pave the way for our children's success or become a stumbling block in their path.

Parental expectations influence every facet of a child's development, from their self-esteem to their stress levels and, ultimately, their well-being. When expectations are balanced and aligned with the child's abilities and interests, they can serve as a powerful motivator. They tell a child, "I believe in you," fostering resilience and a healthy sense of self-worth. However, when these expectations overshoot, landing in unrealistic forms, they can whisper a far less encouraging message: "You're not enough as you are."

Finding the Sweet Spot

The art of parenting lies in finding that sweet spot—a balanced expectation that challenges a child just enough to spur growth without overwhelming them. Imagine a scene from a family movie where a child learns to ride a bike. The parent runs alongside the bike, holding on to the back. There's encouragement, there's support, and importantly, there's a gradual letting go. The child wobbles, maybe even falls, but then comes that magical moment of balance. It's a perfect metaphor for how balanced expectations work. They are about providing support, cheering from the sidelines, and knowing when to let go so the child can find their own balance.

Balanced expectations recognize that each child's developmental journey is unique. They can sprint ahead in some areas while needing extra time to catch up in others. It's akin to customizing the difficulty level of a video game; too easy, and the player loses interest; too hard, and frustration mounts. The goal is to adjust the challenges so they are just right—enough to keep the game engaging without making it unwinnable.

Embracing "Good Enough" Parenting

The idea of good parenting is more appropriately referred to as "realistic and loving parenting." It places a strong emphasis on accepting flaws in children's behavior and accomplishments as well as in parenting techniques. It's a recognition that life, in all its chaotic splendor, deviates from the plan sometimes.

Think of the family comedies where things go hilariously awry—a science project volcano that erupts too soon, a pet that messes up an important dinner, or a DIY home repair that ends in a minor flood. These moments, while exaggerated for comedic effect, remind us of the beauty and bonding that results from imperfection.

"Good enough" parenting is about embracing these less-than-perfect moments as opportunities for growth and connection. It's understanding that the path to a child's success isn't a straight, impeccably paved highway but more of a scenic, winding road, complete with bumps and detours. It's in these detours that children learn resilience, creativity, and the value of effort—lessons that are far more significant than any trophy or grade could ever impart.

This approach doesn't mean lowering our expectations to the point where they no longer inspire or motivate. Rather, it's about setting expectations that are realistic, considering both the child's abilities and the unpredictable nature of growth and learning.

It's knowing that sometimes, the best outcomes come from the least expected sources and that the journey, with all its ups and downs, is as important as the destination.

As parents, our expectations will always be a fundamental part of how we guide and support our children. The key is to wield this tool with care, balancing our aspirations for them with an understanding of their unique journeys and needs. By finding that sweet spot of challenging yet achievable expectations and embracing the concept of "good enough" parenting, we can provide our children with the support, love, and acceptance they need to thrive.

Managing Expectations to Individual Children

Every child is a unique blend of wonder, quirks, and potential. Recognizing and nurturing this individuality is a critical task for every parent. Your family is like a garden, where each child is a different type of plant, requiring its own specific care to thrive. Just as you wouldn't water a cactus with the same frequency as a fern, understanding and adapting to each child's unique temperament, interests, and abilities is essential.

The first step in this journey is observation. Just like Mr. Miyagi in *The Karate Kid*, who seemingly teaches Daniel through chores like waxing cars, you are aiming to discover your child's strengths and areas for growth in everyday activities. Notice how your child interacts with the world: What activities do they gravitate toward? Are they methodical, diving deep into subjects, or do they flit from one interest to another, gathering a broad range of experiences?

Observation isn't just about what they are good at; it's equally about recognizing where they might struggle. It's similar to Peter Parker (Spider-Man) discovering his powers; initially, he has no idea how to control them or what they are good for, but through trial and error, he learns and grows. Likewise, by paying close attention, you can help guide your child through their trials, celebrating their discoveries and supporting their challenges.

Once you have a grasp of your child's temperament and inclinations, the next step is to tailor your expectations to fit their individual profile. Think of this as creating a custom curriculum in the school of life, much like Dumbledore does for Harry in *Harry Potter*, recognizing his unique role and challenges in the wizarding world.

If your child is very interested in music but finds traditional sports difficult, it may be more beneficial to support them in their musical endeavors along with activities that complement their interests. This is not to say you should limit your child only to areas where they naturally excel; challenges are essential for growth. However, recognizing their strengths and areas for growth allows you to set expectations that are both challenging and achievable, much like Yoda's tailored training for Luke Skywalker, which pushes him but is within his reach to master.

Empathy is the foundation of customizing expectations. Remember the scene in *Inside Out* where Joy begins to understand Sadness's role? Just like that moment of insight, seeing the world from your child's perspective can be illuminating. Empathy involves more than just understanding their feelings; it's about deeply comprehending their perspective, motivations, and the way they see the world.

Suppose your child is introverted and feels overwhelmed in large groups; expecting them to be the life of the party or excel in team sports might not be realistic. Instead, understanding their need for quieter, more introspective activities can guide you to encourage participation in clubs or hobbies that honor their nature, like chess, reading groups, or solo sports.

Tailoring expectations might look like setting different bedtimes based on each child's age and needs or encouraging one child to join the debate team while supporting another's interest in solo writing competitions. It's about customizing your parenting approach to fit the individual child, much like how a coach adjusts their strategy based on the strengths and weaknesses of each player on the team.

Adjusting Expectations in Real Time

As your child grows, they will meander through phases, encounter obstacles, and occasionally surprise you by taking an unexpected leap in development. Regularly reviewing and adapting your expectations to fit your child's evolving needs isn't just beneficial—it's essential.

The first rule is to say, "Yes, and..." to whatever scenario is thrown at you, building on it rather than shutting it down. Parenting, much like improv, thrives on flexibility. When your child shifts from a fervent love of dinosaurs to a sudden passion for space overnight, it's your cue to switch themes from *Jurassic Park* to *Interstellar* in your bedtime stories. This adaptability in interests often reflects in your expectations as well. One day, your goal might be for them to identify a T-Rex; the next, to understand gravity. The key is to flow with their current, not against it.

1. Set Regular Check-ins: Just as you might have a family movie night, consider setting aside a "progress chat" night. It doesn't have to be formal; it can be during a meal or a walk. Discuss what has been going well and what challenges have surfaced. This is not a report card session but a chance to understand your child's journey better.

2. Celebrate the Wins, Understand the Losses: Every step forward deserves recognition. Did they finally master tying their shoelaces after switching from Velcro? That's a win. On the flip side, setbacks are not failures but opportunities to learn and grow. If the transition to reading chapter books is taking longer than expected, it's a chance to explore different reading materials or perhaps introduce reading as a shared activity.

3. Stay Curious About Their Interests: When their fascination shifts from painting to playing the guitar, it's an opportunity for growth (for both of you!). Dive into these new interests with them. Who knows? You might find yourself enjoying an impromptu family jam session.

Modeling Flexibility and Adaptability

Children learn a lot from observing their parents. Demonstrating flexibility and adaptability in your daily life teaches you to be resilient and open to change. Here are a few ways to model these behaviors:

- **Show How You Adapt to Changes:** Let's say you planned a picnic, but it rains. Instead of showing disappointment, turn it into an indoor camping adventure. It shows that changes in plans can lead to unexpected fun.

- **Share Your Learning Experiences:** Did a recipe you tried for the first time not turn out as expected? Laugh it off and let your child see that it's okay for things not to go perfectly. Next time, they might share their 'oops' moments more freely, knowing that it's all part of learning.

- **Involve Them in Decision-Making:** When plans need to change, involve your child in finding the solution. It could be as simple as choosing between two indoor activities. This involvement enhances their decision-making skills and shows adaptability is a collective effort.

Regular Reviews: The Family Check-In

Assume that, like the Griswold family in *National Lampoon's Vacation*, you are setting out on a journey. Your end goal is clear (Wally World, in their case), but what is the path? Not so much. Now, parenting isn't always as comedic as a Chevy Chase escapade, but it shares the unpredictability. Regular family check-ins are like pausing at rest stops to review the map. During these moments, ask yourself: How has my child grown? What new interests have they developed? Are there any recent setbacks we need to navigate?

These check-ins don't need to be formal. They can happen over dinner, during bedtime routines, or while building the world's most unstable LEGO tower. The key is to observe and reflect on your child's current stage, not where you assumed they would be.

Flexibility in parenting is similar to being able to pivot from a beach day to a board game marathon because it's suddenly raining cats and dogs. Adaptability is a superpower in the parenting world. It's about adjusting your sails when the wind changes direction. In the classic film *Mrs. Doubtfire*, Daniel Hillard (Robin Williams) doesn't just adapt to his new role with hilarious costume changes; he adjusts his expectations and approach to parenting, learning to balance discipline with love.

To model flexibility for your children, show them it's okay when plans change. If they miss a soccer goal, convince them they can improve as they practice and try again next time. In case their science project didn't go well, at least they have learned about chemical reactions! These moments, framed with humor and grace, teach resilience.

Similarly, teaching them about setbacks is important. In the scene in *Finding Nemo* where Marlin and Dory are swallowed by a whale, Marlin's panic is palpable—it's a parent's worst nightmare. Yet, it's Dory's go-with-the-flow attitude that saves them. The lesson here is not to encourage hitching rides in cetacean mouths but to find the value in setbacks. When your child faces a setback, it's an opportunity to review and adjust your expectations together.

Discuss what happened, not as a failure, but as a learning experience. What can be learned? How can we adjust our approach? Likewise, convince your child to adapt to changes of interest. Imagine if Harry Potter had stuck to the Dursleys' expectation of becoming a mundane, albeit mistreated, clerk instead of embracing his true calling as a wizard. It's quite a different story, but children, much like our favorite characters, evolve. Their interests can change as frequently as the seasons in *Game of Thrones*. One month, it's paleontology; the next, they are aspiring astronauts.

This fluidity is not a challenge but a treasure of childhood. Encourage exploration and be ready to adjust your expectations. Perhaps your envisioned soccer star is more of a chess champion.

Practical Steps for Real-Time Adjustment

1. Set Short-Term Goals: Short-term goals allow for more frequent adjustments and celebrate progress in bite-sized pieces. They are like mini episodes in a long-running series, each with its own arc and development.

2. Maintain Open Communication: Just as in any good buddy movie, communication is key. Regularly chat about interests, goals, and feelings. These conversations can guide your expectation adjustments.

3. Flexibility Drills: Engage in activities that require adaptation. Maybe it's a cooking project that goes awry or a DIY craft that doesn't look anything like the Pinterest picture. Use humor and creativity to find solutions together.

4. Praise the Effort, Not Just the Outcome: Like cheering for every imaginative, albeit plot-hole-ridden, story your child invents, celebrate the process. This reinforces the value of trying and adapting, regardless of the result.

5. Model Positive Adaptation: Let your children see you adapt to changes and setbacks positively. Didn't finish the marathon you trained for? Share your disappointment, but focus on what you learned and how you will adjust your training. Your response teaches resilience and realistic optimism.

Communicating with children can sometimes feel like journeying a complex passage without a map. However, with the right techniques, conveying expectations can become an enlightening journey filled with shared understanding and mutual respect. This section explores how to effectively communicate expectations to your children, ensuring they understand and feel supported in meeting these expectations and guiding them to set their own achievable goals.

Clear and positive communication is the bedrock of setting expectations with children. Instead of saying, "Don't leave your toys everywhere," try, "Please keep your toys in the toybox after playing." It's a simple shift from focusing on the behavior you want to avoid to emphasizing the behavior you desire. Such positive framing encourages cooperation rather than rebellion.

Remember, age-appropriate communication is key. What works for a teenager will not work for a toddler. Break down your expectations into simple, actionable steps for younger children, and offer more detailed explanations to older ones. You may also highlight the reasons behind your expectations.

As your child grows, so will their ability to meet different expectations. It's important to recognize and adjust these expectations accordingly. It's like how Andy's mom in *Toy Story* understands that he's outgrown his toys, symbolizing a shift in his interests and capabilities. You may regularly check with your child to discuss what's working and what isn't, and be willing to adjust your expectations as they grow.

Dealing with Unmet Expectations

Every parent dreams of their child achieving greatness—hitting every milestone with precision, excelling in every field they venture into, and basically, being the embodiment of success. However, as the journey of parenting unravels, it becomes evident that these dreams often hit snags, and expectations, more often than not, go unmet. The road is not always smooth, and it's filled with unexpected turns, much like the plot of a family adventure movie where the heroes find themselves facing challenges they hadn't anticipated but emerge stronger from them.

When children fail to meet our expectations, it's not just a test of their resilience but ours, too. This chapter aims to guide you through these moments with practical strategies, emphasizing the silver lining in every cloud of unmet expectations.

Learning from Failure: The Importance of Resilience

In *Kung Fu Panda*, Po's journey from clumsy panda to the Dragon Warrior is filled with setbacks. Yet, with each failure, he learns and grows stronger. This story exemplifies the importance of resilience—the ability to bounce back from failure. Teach your child that failure is not the opposite of success but a part of the success story.

One of the most heartwarming scenes in *Harry Potter* is when Dumbledore tells Harry that it is our choices that show what we truly are, far more than our abilities. This sentiment is crucial when adjusting expectations. Make sure your child understands that their worth is not tied to their achievements. Reinforce the idea that while goals might change, their value as a person does not diminish. It's like adjusting the sails on a boat to catch the wind better; you are merely changing the approach, not the destination.

Creating a Family Culture that Values Perseverance

So, how do we create a family culture that applauds the journey as much as the destination? It begins with our own attitudes toward success and failure. By sharing our own stories of effort, especially those sprinkled with humor and humility from our own lives or even favorite family movies, we can demonstrate that it's normal to face setbacks and that persistence is key.

Start by praising the process rather than the outcome. For example, instead of saying, "Great job on getting an A," try, "I'm really proud of how hard you studied and how you kept going, even when the material was challenging." This subtle shift in focus highlights the importance of effort and the learning process itself.

Remember to celebrate the small wins along the way. Did your child spend more time on their homework tonight? Did they try again after a setback? These moments deserve recognition. You can even create family rituals around celebrating effort like a special dinner, every time someone in the family demonstrates exceptional perseverance.

Encourage your children to reflect on their efforts and the progress they have made. Ask them what they learned from the experience and what they might do differently next time. This reflection not only reinforces the value of effort but also helps them internalize what they learn from each challenge.

Last but not least, embrace imperfection. Let your children see you tackle new challenges and make mistakes. Watching you handle setbacks with grace and humor shows them that it's okay not to be perfect and that what matters most is the effort we put in and the lessons we learn along the way.

The heart of the message lies in the significance of setting realistic expectations. Such expectations serve not just as guidelines for behavior and growth but as a foundation for nurturing a positive and enriching parent-child relationship. It's about striking a balance—challenging our children to reach their potential while also respecting their individuality and current capabilities.

Parenting, in essence, is a journey—one that is filled with moments of joy, frustration, laughter, and learning. It requires patience, understanding, and a whole lot of love. As we strive to set realistic expectations for our children, we also learn to adjust our own expectations for ourselves as parents. We are reminded that perfection is not the goal; rather, it's the continuous effort to understand, support, and guide our children as they grow into their unique selves.

Chapter 12: Patience in the Digital Age

Guess who is winning in the race between technology and childhood? If you said technology, you are not alone. You can now commonly witness a toddler swiping a magazine like a tablet, puzzled why it doesn't change pages. It's a funny thing, but it perfectly captures how the digital age has changed the playground rules.

Gone are the days when waiting for your favorite cartoon or the anticipation of a handwritten letter was the norm. Today's children are growing up in a world where almost everything is a click away. The magic of the internet, for all its wonders, has introduced a new challenge for parents: teaching patience in a world that moves faster than a speedy internet connection.

This makes patience feel like a rare commodity these days. A world where dinner doesn't come from a microwave, messages take more than a second to deliver, and you actually have to wait for the next episode of your favorite show until next week. Does it sound like a plot from a historical novel? Well, that was reality not too long ago. Now, we live in a time where waiting more than two seconds for a video to buffer feels like an eternity.

This shift isn't just about convenience; it's fundamentally changing how young minds develop expectations and understand the concept of waiting. The significance of teaching patience today cannot be overstated. It's like trying to teach someone to swim in a pool that's constantly in motion. But fear not! The digital world, with all its gifs, TikToks, and instant messages, also provides a unique opportunity to teach patience in ways that resonate with the tech-savvy generation.

For instance, have you ever noticed how a video game can teach a child to persist through challenges until they reach the next level? It's patience in disguise! Or consider the child who saves up virtual coins for a prized in-game item. That's delayed gratification with a digital twist. The key is to use these moments as stepping stones to broader lessons about patience.

But let's be honest, teaching patience in an age of instant gratification is a bit like trying to keep socks on a toddler – it seems nearly impossible, but with perseverance, creativity, and a sense of humor, it can be done. We will explore how setting screen time limits can be a game of strategy rather than a battlefield, turning frustration into laughter when the Wi-Fi takes a sudden vacation.

So, as we embark on this journey to instill the virtue of patience in our children, remember, it's not about removing technology from their lives. It's about guiding them to use it wisely, understanding its limits, and finding joy in the moments in between. After all, some of life's best moments happen in the waiting. Like the anticipation before the first snowfall, or the suspense of a paused video game level – these moments teach us that good things come to those who wait, even in the digital age.

The Quest for the Golden Notification

Imagine a scenario where young Tommy is playing his favorite video game online. He is on a critical mission that requires utmost concentration and patience. But then, his phone buzzes with a notification. It's a like on his recent social media post! Suddenly, the critical mission seems less important than checking who appreciated his culinary experiment with a microwave burrito. This isn't just about loss of focus; it reflects the diminishing attention spans and impulse control in children and adolescents, thanks in no small part to digital media consumption.

Research findings suggest that the constant barrage of notifications, likes, and messages is shortening our attention spans and making it harder for us to wait, concentrate, and control impulses. It's as if every ping and buzz trains our brains to expect immediate rewards, sidelining the sweet virtue of patience.

The Great Paradox of Connectivity

On one hand, digital tools have brought us closer than ever before. Grandma can see her grandkids' first steps in real-time, halfway across the globe. Yet, this same connectivity breeds a sense of urgency and impatience. Why has not Grandma replied to the video yet? Is she not impressed with the gravity-defying act of taking those first steps?

This paradox is a tricky beast. We are more connected but also more impatient, expecting instantaneous responses to our digital interactions. It's like we are all part of a global game of digital tag, where being "it" lasts only until the next notification.

Consider the story of Sarah, a diligent student who decided to email her teacher at midnight about a pressing question on her homework. When she did not receive a reply by 1 a.m., Sarah was convinced her academic future was in jeopardy. This story isn't just proof of Sarah's dedication but illustrates how digital expectations have seeped into our perception of time and patience. The idea that everything, including responses, should come instantly is a significant departure from the pre-digital era's norms.

So, what can we do to help our young digital natives navigate these choppy waters? First, we can start by setting examples. Just like the mythical creatures of old who could resist the siren calls, we too can show resilience against the allure of the instant notification. Maybe, just maybe, we can resist the urge to check our phones at dinner or during family game night.

We can also encourage activities that don't come with a power button. Remember those? Books, board games, and the great outdoors still exist, offering endless opportunities for learning patience and enjoying the moment without a digital interruption. And when we do use digital devices (because they're not going anywhere), we can do so with intention. Teach the value of thoughtful responses over rapid-fire texts. Encourage waiting periods before reacting to emails or comments. It's about bringing back the art of reflection in our fast-paced digital dialogue.

For you as parents, keeping up with the latest digital trends can feel a bit like trying to brush your teeth while eating Oreos: messy, counterintuitive, and with a high chance of leaving you feeling slightly bewildered. Yet, understanding the digital playground your kids frolic in daily is a crucial step toward teaching them patience in an age where everything is just a click away.

If you have ever noticed your teenager taking selfies with the intensity of a National Geographic photographer, you are witnessing the social media effect. Platforms like Instagram, TikTok, and Snapchat have turned everyday life into a highlight reel. While there is nothing inherently wrong with sharing and connecting, the instant feedback loop of likes and comments can set unrealistic expectations for immediate gratification and constant entertainment.

Then there are video games, a universe where dragons are slain, goals are scored, and kingdoms are built before dinner time. Video games are not the enemy; in fact, they can enhance problem-solving skills and hand-eye coordination. However, the immediate rewards and continuous action can make the real world, where achievements take time and effort, seem painfully slow in comparison.

Instant messaging deserves a mention too. Remember passing notes in class? Today's kids have WhatsApp, Messenger, and a slew of other messaging apps. While instant messaging has made communication wonderfully convenient, it also teaches kids to expect immediate responses, making the virtue of patience seem like a relic of the past.

The digital world is shaping how our kids think, interact, and expect the world to respond to them.

They are growing up in a reality where boredom is rare, and entertainment is endless, a stark contrast to the days of dial-up internet and "outside" being the main source of amusement.

But it's not all doom and gloom. This digital world also offers fertile ground for teaching patience. Imagine the comedic potential of explaining to a child that once upon a time, people had to go to a store to rent a movie, and if someone else had borrowed it first, you just had to wait. Or the incredulous looks you might receive when you describe how, in the dark ages before smartphones, if you wanted to know something, you had to look it up in an encyclopedia or *gasp* ask a real human being and wait for an answer.

Steering the digital world with your kids offers endless opportunities for teaching moments on patience. It's about finding balance, like limiting screen time but also sitting down to play a video game with them, showing that some quests take time to complete. It's about encouraging them to post on social media but also discussing the value of in-person connections that don't offer instant feedback.

Thus, understanding the digital world your children inhabit is like learning to speak their language. It's not always easy, and you might feel like you are butchering the accent, but the effort shows your kids that you are trying to see the world from their viewpoint. And in those shared moments of discovery and discussion, you are not just teaching patience; you are building bridges.

Screen Time Vs. Scream Time

The American Academy of Pediatrics (AAP) and the World Health Organization (WHO) didn't pull their recommendations out of thin air. They have done the legwork so you don't have to, providing a roadmap for the digital jungle. For toddlers aged 2 to 5, the golden rule is one hour per day. Before you laugh and say, 'Sure, and I'm the Tooth Fairy,' consider this as more of a goal than a strict rule. For kids six and older, the guidelines become a bit more flexible, focusing on the quality of content rather than the ticking clock. But what is the bottom line? Less is usually more.

Now, enforcing these limits can be as challenging as getting a cat to walk on a leash. Take, for example, the story of Jimmy, who would turn into a mini-Hulk every time the iPad was pried from his not-so-tiny hands. What is the solution to it? His parents introduced what they affectionately called 'The Great Swap.' For every hour spent outside pretending to be a dinosaur, Jimmy earned 15 minutes of screen time. The backyard suddenly became the Mesozoic era, and peace was restored to the household.

But important thing is, setting these boundaries isn't just about preventing your child from becoming a screen zombie; it's about encouraging them to explore the world in 3D. The real one, with dirt, and trees, and those things called 'books.' It's about helping them discover that boredom is actually the secret ingredient to creativity. Remember, every great inventor, artist, and thinker got there by staring out of the window, not at a screen.

The importance of setting and enforcing screen time limits goes beyond preventing square eyes—it's about fostering healthier digital habits that will stick with them into adulthood. Like eating broccoli or brushing teeth, it might not always be fun, but it is necessary.

The story of Lisa fits best in this regard. Lisa implemented a 'tech-free Tuesday' in her household. The first few weeks were tough; complaints flew like confetti at a parade. But soon, something magical happened. The family started playing board games, rediscovering the lost art of conversation, and actually looking forward to these digital detox days. Lisa's family learned that screen time limits weren't a punishment but a passport to rediscovering each other.

So, as a parent, remember that setting screen time guidelines isn't about depriving your little ones of fun. It's about giving them the gift of time—time to play, to dream, and to just be kids. And who knows, you might just find yourself rediscovering the joy of living unplugged at least, until next day rolls around.

Strategies for Balancing Technology and Patience

In the age where digital devices are almost like extra limbs, teaching patience to our kids can feel like trying to keep a cat entertained without a laser pointer. Yet, as challenging as it might seem, striking a balance between technology and patience is not only possible but can also be quite fun.

First, the power of creating a balanced digital environment at home is enormous. It can make your home, a haven where technology and simplicity coexist in harmony. This sounds peaceful, but here's a simple start—have a charging station outside of bedrooms, making it the pit stop for devices during the night. This not only ensures better sleep but also subtly teaches your kids that life can go on, quite wonderfully, without being glued to a screen till the crack of dawn.

Now, onto the magic of tech-free times and zones. Visualize your dining table as a tiny island where no digital device dares to tread. Meals become opportunities for conversations about anything under the sun, from how bananas get their spots to why the sky is blue. These moments, free from digital interruptions, teach patience and the joy of human connection.

Encouraging offline activities is like rediscovering the lost art of treasure hunting, but instead of gold, you are hunting for patience. Swap screen time with activities like reading, where the only scroll is turning a page, or puzzles that don't solve themselves with a few taps. Board games are another great swap, turning potential screen zombies into enthusiastic strategists. Here's a hilarious idea: have you ever witnessed someone attempt to speed a puzzle? It's similar to attempting to rush a snail; both are pointless activities that unintentionally teach patience.

And finally, let's discuss your hidden weapon: co-viewing or co-playing. This is where you go into the digital world with your kids, but instead of just passively watching, you engage with them. Ask questions about the game they are playing or the show they are watching. It's a bit like being a detective, but instead of solving crimes, you are uncovering the storyline and the thinking behind certain digital decisions. This not only helps you understand the content but also sparks critical thinking in your child. Think of it as the modern version of reading a book together, where the discussions about character motives are replaced with why certain characters in games make the choices they do.

Incorporating these strategies into your family life doesn't require a complete digital detox but rather a mindful approach to technology use. By setting these guidelines, you're not only teaching your children patience but also showing them that there's a vast, exciting world beyond screens. And who knows? In the process, you might rediscover some of your own childhood joys, proving that patience truly is a virtue, especially in our fast-paced digital world.

Fostering Mindful Digital Consumption

Imagine that your child is about to go headfirst into the digital ocean. But instead of letting them swim with just any fish, you equip them with a digital snorkel that guides them to the most colorful reefs. This is what teaching mindfulness in digital consumption looks like. It's about helping your child recognize the difference between mindlessly gobbling up digital junk food and savoring the nourishing bits of the internet.

Technique 1: The Preview Pause

Before letting your child watch a new show or play a new game, take a moment to preview it together. Ask questions like, "What do you think this is about?" or "Do you think this will be a fun way to learn something new?" This isn't just about making sure the content is appropriate; it's about encouraging your child to think critically about what they consume digitally.

Technique 2: The Active Engagement Experiment

Turn passive screen time into an interactive adventure. If they are watching a documentary about sea life? Why not draw your favorite sea creature together afterward? If they are playing an educational game? Set challenges for each other based on the game's content. By engaging actively with digital media, children learn to value quality over quantity.

Now, onto the holy grail of modern parenting: teaching patience in an age when even toasters have a fast-forward button. The key here is to turn waiting into a game itself, one that's just as fun as the digital delights on the other side of that wait.

Create a waiting game for any situation where impatience typically rears its head. A new app about to be downloaded? Together, let's estimate how many seconds it will take. Awaiting the beginning of a video? Until it starts, set a challenge for your youngster to balance on one foot. These minigames not only teach important lessons about patience, but they also make waiting enjoyable.

Remember, little eyes are always watching. Show your child what digital patience looks like. Is a website taking forever to load? Take a deep breath and share a quick story about a time when waiting paid off for you. Your reaction to digital waits teaches your child more about patience than any lesson or lecture ever could.

By incorporating these strategies into your digital routine, you'll help your child navigate the vast sea of the internet with mindfulness and patience. And who knows? You might just find that these lessons in digital consumption enrich your own digital experiences as well.

Addressing Challenges

Enforcing digital patience at home feels like trying to herd cats. It's tricky, but not impossible. One common challenge is the sheer persistence of kids when they want more screen time. You say, "Only 30 minutes of video games," and somehow, it turns into a mini-series of negotiations worthy of a courtroom drama. What is the key? Stay firm but fair. It's like being a benevolent dictator of digital time. Consistency is your best friend here. Stick to the agreed-upon rules, and eventually, the message gets through: no amount of puppy eyes or bargaining will change the law of the land.

And then there's the skill of persistence. Let's say you have a policy prohibiting electronics during dinner, but suddenly you hear the frantic buzz of a message. It's tempting to let it slide "just this once," but doing so is like opening the floodgates. Instead, try turning it into a game: the first one to reach for their phone does the dishes. You might end up with the cleanest plates in the neighborhood, but it's for a good cause.

The Role of Schools and Educators

Now, schools have a part to play too. They are like the second line of defense in the quest for digital patience. Imagine a classroom where, instead of banning devices outright, teachers use them as tools for learning about digital citizenship. It's about teaching kids not just how to use technology, but how to use it wisely and patiently. Schools can set up scenarios where students must wait their turn to contribute to a digital project, teaching patience naturally in the process.

Educators can also be invaluable allies in reinforcing the digital boundaries you set at home. Through policies and education around screen time, they help children understand that there is a time to swipe and scroll and a time to learn and interact face-to-face. It's the academic equivalent of teaching kids that eating vegetables is part of a balanced diet—not always fun, but good for them.

Encouraging Positive Digital Interactions

Encouraging positive digital interactions is like guiding children through a minefield of distractions and instant gratifications. It's teaching them that not every email marked urgent requires an immediate response, and that crafting a thoughtful message is more rewarding than firing off a quick, emoji-laden reply. One strategy is to practice drafting responses together, turning it into a fun activity rather than a chore. Think of it as teaching your child to be a digital poet, where every word is chosen with care and intention.

Similarly, teaching patience in a digital world is about finding balance. It's a blend of setting boundaries, being consistent, and leading by example. It's not always easy; it is more like convincing a cat to take a leisurely swim. However, with a dash of creativity and a dollop of perseverance, it's definitely within reach. Who knows? You might just find yourself enjoying the process, one sunny, lazy, patience-building Sunday at a time.

So, expecting a child to understand the value of patience without guidance is like expecting a dog to pass up a dropped piece of steak. Unlikely, surely? Here's where you fit in. Your role in fostering patience is akin to teaching them how to ride a bike. At first, there is a lot of wobbling, a few crashes, and maybe even some tears. But with your support, encouragement, and the occasional nudge in the right direction, they will be cruising smoothly, enjoying the ride.

The digital world, with all its pings, pops, and buzzes, is a veritable jungle gym of distractions. However, as you continue this journey of teaching patience, remember to celebrate the victories, no matter how small. If they managed to wait an extra minute before checking the phone? That is a win. If they chose to read a book while waiting, instead of mindlessly scrolling? Pop the non-literal champagne. These moments are the building blocks of patience and deserve a high-five or a happy dance.

Therefore, we must remind ourselves that teaching patience in a world wired for speed is not just an act of love; it's an investment in our children's future. It equips them with the ability to pause, reflect, and engage deeply with the world around them. So, here's to you, the parents, educators, and caregivers, for taking on this challenge. Your efforts to instill patience today are creating a more thoughtful, mindful, and resilient generation for tomorrow. And remember, every time you successfully teach a moment of patience, somewhere out there, a cat is considering the benefits of a leisurely swim.

Chapter 13: Collaboration with Teachers and Caregivers

In the living time, patience is not just a virtue; it's a necessity that holds upbringing together, ensuring that as children grow, they learn to work through their emotions, understand the value of waiting, and appreciate the art of persistence. However, teaching patience is not a task that falls on the shoulders of parents alone. It's a collective effort, one that requires the collaboration of everyone involved in a child's life, from parents to teachers to the broader circle of caregivers. It is impossible to overstate the importance of this cohesive approach since it is essential to children's overall development of patience and other vital qualities.

Imagine a scenario where a child hears about the importance of waiting from their parents at home, experiences the benefits of patience through activities in school, and observes patience in action through the behaviors of their caregivers. This consistent reinforcement across different spheres of their life doesn't just teach them patience; it embeds it into their understanding of how the world works.

However, achieving this level of consistency is easier said than done. It requires more than just a common goal; it necessitates a shared strategy and ongoing communication between all parties involved. The concept of consistency across different environments and its impact on children's learning and behavior is pivotal. Children, with their keen observational skills and inherent adaptability, are quick to pick up on discrepancies between what they are told at home and what they experience outside. If a child is encouraged to practice patience at home but finds themselves in environments where instant gratification is the norm, the mixed messages can be confusing and counterproductive.

To bring this point home, consider the amusing fact that even animals display remarkable patience when trained consistently. Studies have shown that crows can wait patiently for better rewards if they have learned that patience pays off—somewhat akin to children learning to wait an extra minute for a double scoop of ice cream instead of settling for a single scoop right away. The lesson here is that consistency is key, whether we are dealing with humans or birds.

In a "Marshmallow Test" the children who could wait 15 minutes to get two marshmallows instead of eating one immediately weren't just showcasing their budding patience. They were demonstrating what consistent guidance and practice in patience can achieve, even if it's just for the sweet reward of an extra marshmallow. It's a light-hearted reminder that the lessons in patience we teach, and the consistency with which we teach them, can have long-lasting effects on our children's futures.

The Role of Teachers and Caregivers in Children's Development

Teachers and caregivers are akin to gardeners tending to their plants. Just as a gardener provides the right balance of sunlight, water, and nutrients, educators and caregivers offer the emotional and social sustenance that children need to grow. Did you know that children are more likely to attempt new challenges and persevere after witnessing their teachers handle tasks with patience and determination? This is because children often model their behavior after adults they trust and admire.

These pivotal figures play a crucial role in reinforcing the values and behaviors taught at home. For instance, when a teacher practices patience by calmly addressing a student's mistake, it echoes the patience a parent shows at home when their child spills milk for the umpteenth time. These moments, though seemingly small, are monumental in teaching children the importance of patience through consistent examples set by both their home and educational environments.

The concept of "It takes a village to raise a child" rings especially true in the context of teaching patience. The combined efforts of parents, teachers, and caregivers in presenting a unified front of expectations, discipline, and patience create a secure and supportive environment for children to learn and grow. But how exactly can this be achieved?

First, communication is key. It's like building a bridge between home and school/daycare. Without it, you are just shouting across the river and hoping for the best. Parents taking the initiative to establish open lines of communication with teachers and caregivers is akin to setting the foundation stones for this bridge. This could be as simple as scheduling regular meetings to discuss the child's progress or using a shared diary to note observations and behaviors. Remember, the goal here is not to create a surveillance state but to foster a partnership based on mutual respect and shared objectives.

Penguins are known for their incredible patience, taking turns to stand in the bitter cold to protect their eggs. While we are not suggesting that you stand in the cold, there's something to be learned from our feathered friends about taking turns and sharing responsibilities in the nurturing process. Just like penguins, parents, teachers, and caregivers can take turns reinforcing patience, each playing their role at different times and settings to provide a cohesive learning experience for the child.

To make this collaboration even more effective, try implementing shared strategies and approaches to teaching patience. This doesn't mean that every minor detail has to be identical in both environments. Rather, it's about agreeing on the core principles and adapting them to fit each setting. For instance, if a child is learning about waiting their turn at school through group activities, a similar approach can be applied at home during family game night.

In the end, the harmonious collaboration between parents, teachers, and caregivers in teaching patience and other virtues is similar to a well-conducted orchestra. Each member plays their part, contributing to the child's development. It's about creating a consistent and supportive backdrop against which children can learn the valuable lessons of patience, perseverance, and empathy.

Communication Strategies for Effective Collaboration

First off, let's talk about communication. It's the bedrock of any successful collaboration, but let's be honest, sometimes it feels less like a bedrock and more like a stumbling block, especially when we are trying to sync up with busy teachers and caregivers who have their own sets of priorities and concerns.

The idea of "regular meetings" might induce a collective groan. Imagine trying to find a time that works for everyone, only to end up discussing why Timmy won't eat his peas. Yet, these meetings are crucial. They don't have to be formal sit-downs that last hours; they could be as simple as a 10-minute catch-up after drop-off or a brief phone call every other week. The aim here is to keep the lines of communication open, ensuring everyone is on the same page.

Then there are shared tools—communication books, apps, and even the good old email chain. Think of these as your baton in the relay race of caregiving. These tools can help pass along vital information about your child's day, their mood swings, victories, and meltdowns. It's like being handed a script each day, helping you understand your child's narrative in the absence of firsthand experience.

Did you know there's an app for just about everything these days? Including one that can remind you to water your plants. If we can have that, surely we can utilize apps to foster better communication about our children's development. Let's not let the plant apps show us up.

Creating Consistency Across Environments

The next piece of the puzzle is ensuring consistency across various environments. This is crucial because children, much like adults, thrive on consistency. It's confusing if jumping on the bed is allowed at Grandma's but it is a cardinal sin at home.

Creating a unified front means ensuring that the messages we send about patience and behavior are the same, no matter where the child is. For instance, if patience is rewarded with positive reinforcement at home, the same should apply at school. This doesn't mean that everyone needs to become clones of each other in their approach, but the core message should remain consistent.

Think of it as a franchise restaurant. Whether you walk into a McDonald's in New York or New Delhi, you expect the Big Mac to taste the same. Similarly, your child should receive the same flavor of guidance, irrespective of the caregiver or teacher they are with.

Synchronizing Routines and Expectations

Synchronizing routines and expectations across different environments can be similar to conducting an orchestra where each musician plays a different instrument. The idea is to create a masterpiece, not a cacophony. This might involve setting similar boundaries and routines regarding homework, screen time, and even bedtime rituals.

There's a family that implemented a "no screen time" rule during weekdays. The grandmother, however, thought this rule was more of a guideline than an actual rule. The children quickly realized that Grandma's house was an anarchic paradise where rules went to die. It took several family meetings and the promise of more cookies than was probably wise to bring Grandma into the fold. Now, she's the fiercest enforcer of the no-screen rule!

Dealing with Discrepancies in Approaches

Imagine you are a jazz musician. Your style is all about improvisation, flowing with the vibe. Your child's teacher, on the other hand, might be more of a classical musician, favoring structure and precision. Both styles create beautiful music, but they are different. Similarly, your approach to teaching patience and handling behavior may not always match up perfectly with that of your child's teacher or caregiver.

First off, let's acknowledge that these discrepancies are not only normal but expected. After all, diversity is the spice of life. It introduces our children to various ways of learning and adapting, which is a lesson in patience. However, when these differences crop up, it's like hitting a sour note in our harmonious endeavor. The key here is not to ignore it but to tune our instruments and find a melody that works for everyone involved.

Here's a piece of advice as timeless as the abacus: Communication is king. Engage in open, respectful conversations with your child's teacher or caregiver. Share your observations and concerns without the finger-pointing. Remember, it's not you vs. them; it's all of you for the child. Bring to the table what you've noticed works at home, and be open to hearing their professional insights. This exchange is not just beneficial; it's a goldmine of opportunities to learn and grow together.

When you do find discrepancies, approach them with a problem-solving mindset. Think of it as assembling a piece of IKEA furniture without the instructions. You both have the same goal but might have different ideas about how to get there. Maybe there's a compromise, a hybrid approach that combines the best of both worlds. Or perhaps, through discussion, one of you will have an "aha" moment, realizing the other's method addresses something you hadn't considered.

Role of Parents in Supporting Teachers and Caregivers

Supporting teachers and caregivers doesn't just enhance parents' ability to teach patience; it reinforces a network of consistency and understanding around the child, which is as crucial as the air we breathe.

Volunteering in your child's classroom or daycare can be an eye-opener. It's like being a fly on the wall, but less creepy and far more helpful. You get a front-row seat to the teacher's strategies in action, the classroom dynamics, and how your child interacts in a group setting. This insight is invaluable, providing a clearer picture and fostering a deeper appreciation for the educator's role and challenges. Plus, your presence sends a clear message to your child that you are part of a team, working with the teacher, not against them.

Providing resources might sound like we suggest showing up with a trunk full of gold coins. While that would make you very popular, it's not quite what we mean. Resources can be as simple as sharing articles, books, or materials that you have found helpful. It could also mean contributing to the classroom— perhaps through materials that aid in teaching patience and emotional regulation, like books, games, or calming tools.

Showing appreciation is, quite frankly, a superpower. A heartfelt "thank you" can turn a day around. Teachers and caregivers are human, and like anyone else, they thrive on acknowledgment and appreciation. It could be as simple as a note, a small gift, or a public shout-out during a PTA meeting. Recognizing their hard work and dedication not only boosts morale but strengthens the bond between you and them.

Lastly, backing up educators' strategies and decisions in front of your child is crucial. Imagine if Batman and Robin argued about how to catch the Joker in front of him. It is not very effective, right? Consistency between home and school/care settings reinforces authority and teaches respect. If you have concerns about a strategy or decision, discuss it privately with the educator. Present a united front publicly. This doesn't mean blind agreement but rather a cohesive approach to supporting your child's learning and development.

Community Workshops and Seminars

You might not turn green and rip your clothes every time you're tested (hopefully), but the frustration is real. Workshops and Seminars are gold mines for learning new strategies and understanding that your challenges aren't unique. The person sitting next to you might have just stopped themselves from launching a toy train into orbit after the hundredth viewing of "The Little Engine That Could." Sharing these moments can be both enlightening and hilariously reassuring.

Workshops offer hands-on experiences where you can practice patience in real-time, often with professionals who can guide you through the Hulk moments without turning green. They provide tools, role-playing scenarios, and strategies that you can tailor to fit your family's needs. It's like getting a custom-made patience toolkit, with the added bonus of being able to ask questions and get immediate feedback. Plus, you can witness firsthand that the technique that worked wonders on taming your neighbor's tantrum-throwing toddler might also work on your little angel.

Support Groups: The Parental Bat-Signal

Now, onto support groups, or as I like to call them, the parental Bat-Signal. These are the beacons for when you are two minutes away from scheduling a parent-teacher conference to suggest that they introduce nap time for parents. Support groups provide a space to vent, share, and receive advice in a judgment-free zone. It's like having a group of friends who won't blink an eye when you share that your child's latest tantrum was over the unacceptable shape of their toast.

These groups often share resources like articles, books, and sometimes guest speakers, ranging from child psychologists to seasoned parents with a sense of humor sharper than a LEGO you stepped on at midnight. The beauty of these groups is the realization that you are not alone in your quest for patience. There is a communal sigh of relief in discovering that your child isn't the only one who can cry for hours over the mysterious disappearance of their imaginary friend's pet rock.

The Ripple Effect of Community Involvement

Community involvement has a ripple effect that benefits not just parents but also children, teachers, and caregivers. When parents learn new strategies for patience, this doesn't just stay within the family home; it extends to how they interact with teachers and caregivers, creating a more cohesive and understanding approach to dealing with challenges. It's similar to a group project where everyone is finally on the same page, and miraculously, the project succeeds (and no one even threatened to quit the group).

Seeing adults in their lives come together in this way can be incredibly reassuring for children. It reinforces the idea that they are supported not just by their family but by a whole community. It's the difference between facing a scary monster alone and turning around to find an entire squad armed with patience and understanding (and maybe some chocolate).

Benefits of Community Involvement

The benefits of community involvement are numerous. For starters, it can significantly reduce the feeling of isolation that many parents face. It's comforting to know that there's a network of people who not only understand your struggles but can also laugh and cry with you about them. This sense of belonging can be a powerful antidote to the stress and frustration that often accompany parenting.

Furthermore, community resources often provide access to a wide range of expertise to help you navigate the complexities of raising children. From learning how to communicate effectively with your kids to managing your own stress levels, these resources can offer invaluable insights and practical advice.

Finally, being part of a community fosters a sense of contribution and satisfaction. Sharing your own experiences and strategies can help others feel less alone, creating a positive feedback loop where everyone benefits.

The journey to cultivate patience is a marathon, not a sprint. It requires persistence, a pinch of humor, and a heap of teamwork. Think of it as assembling a complex piece of IKEA furniture without the instruction manual. At first, it seems daunting, perhaps impossible. But with communication, collaboration, and a few laughs over misplaced screws, what once seemed like a pile of unrelated pieces comes together to form a sturdy, functional, and beautiful structure. Similarly, by working together, we build the framework within which our children learn the value of patience.

In closing, remember that every effort you make, every conversation you have, and every strategy you implement is a step toward nurturing a more patient, understanding, and resilient generation. So, let's keep those lines of communication wide open, maintain consistency across all fronts, and maybe, just maybe, keep an extra pancake on hand, just in case. Here's to not just teaching patience but living it, one pancake-flipping, baton-passing, furniture-assembling day at a time.

Chapter 14: Celebrating Milestones

I believe there is nothing more amazing than becoming a parent to an adorable little human who looks up to you in a way you could never have imagined. That's right, parenthood is amazing on so many levels.

The best part is the unconditional love that comes into your life. Seeing your child smile for the first time, holding your hand with their tiny fingers, and taking the first steps are experiences you cherish forever. Moreover, sharing some trivial yet memorable moments with your children as they look at the world with their fresh eyes are pleasures that cannot be verbalized.

Showing your child a ladybug, or helping them cross a puddle are things you treasure. On a personal level, knowing that a little soul looks up to you encourages you to become a better version of yourself. You also become aware of the qualities you didn't know existed.

However, there is nothing more satisfying than witnessing your child's milestone. I think no matter how old people get, there is nothing that can keep their parents from seeing them as the cute little angel they were on their first day on this earth. From seeing your kid start school to the day they get a PhD degree, celebrating their triumphs brings you a special kind of pride, which is different from all the proud moments you have lived in your life.

But why are these milestones so important? Ever thought about that? Well, if you ask me, the simplest answer I can provide is that these milestones are nothing less than a testament to your child's growth, the resilience they will develop going forth, as well as the individuals they will grow up to be.

To begin with, when we celebrate our kids' milestones, we make them realize that their accomplishments matter, regardless of how little they may appear to the world. It shows them how important their efforts, their hard work, and their determination are. This gives them a feeling that they are seen, heard, cherished, and loved. Such gestures keep them in higher spirits while shaping their individuality for the better and allowing them to become confident individuals growing up.

The confidence we help them develop through appreciation and acknowledgment aids them to deal better with life's challenges. Contrary to popular belief, celebrating a child's milestone is far more than throwing them a party. It would be great if you did, but it is a lot more than that. Let's delve deeper and discuss in detail some of the benefits of celebrating their milestones.

The 'I Did It' Moment

When we celebrate a child's accomplishments or even their efforts regardless of how big or small they are, their little brains release dopamine, a feel good chemical, which allows them to cultivate a positive association with achievement. As a result, they tend to crave and anticipate the feeling of accomplishment once again.

Suppose your child learns to tie their shoelaces. Words like "attaboy" or "good job" can go a long way. Moreover, the dopamine rush can boost their confidence, thus encouraging them to take on similar tasks.

This is where you see the power of recognition. Consider your child building a tower with Lego blocks. When you appreciate their efforts with words like, "Wow! This is higher than I expected," you are actually telling them, "You have done a fabulous job. I am proud of you." Such words provide them with a sense of self-worth and make them feel capable of achieving great things. When they know their efforts are appreciated, they tend to develop healthy self-esteem.

Milestones Are Stepping Stones

Milestones are stepping stones that eventually guide a person to a much bigger goal. By celebrating the smaller wins, you encourage and motivate the children to keep moving forward with their goals. Suppose your child has been practicing the guitar, and after they have mastered the chords, they are finally beginning to play licks, which is a challenging task for a beginning guitarist.

By telling them things like "Wow! You have really aced that part," you ensure that they stay enthusiastic about going all the way and not quitting halfway through. Another great thing about words of encouragement and appreciation is that they teach the kids how significant progress is.

Such a mindset is crucially essential when children are faced with challenges and obstacles. Children who are appreciated tend to grow up with a growth mindset as opposed to a fixed mindset. They realize that skills and talents can continuously be developed and improved and that challenges are opportunities for growth.

The "Yet" Mindset

The "yet" mindset instills in your child the power of perseverance. It also teaches them that their milestones aren't about perfection, but progress. Celebrating small wins makes the child motivated, and allows them to realize that they are yet to achieve the feat they are truly capable of.

Your child might be struggling to ride a bike, and might be falling off every now and then. Do not discourage them by showing signs of frustration. Cheering for every time they ride without falling off will help them realize that they are making steady progress, but they are yet to learn to ride without making mistakes. They will stay poised to keep trying until they master it.

The "yet" mindset also gives them the feeling that they are almost there. Suppose your child is solving a complex puzzle, and has successfully managed to complete 70% of it, while failing for the remaining 30%. A few words of encouragement will tell them they are almost there so they continue striving for the bigger goal, which is to complete the puzzle. The best thing is that the "yet" mindset makes them subconsciously rule out the possibility of quitting.

Building a Support System

Celebrating a child's milestone leads to a village effect. This village effect gives the child the feeling that there is a strong support system backing him up. They feel surrounded by people who love them, care for them, and appreciate their efforts. You can make your child read a story book before the family after he has learnt to read. It would certainly be a moment of excitement for them, which makes the child want to learn new things, while creating for them a healthy learning environment.

Moreover, sharing joyful moments with milestones results in a sense of belonging and connection. For example, showcasing your child's art piece on your refrigerator makes them realize that their efforts are acknowledged and appreciated by the whole family. The whole exercise makes the child understand the importance of community, and the encouragement they receive makes them want to continue their work, thus taking their craft to a whole new level.

Reinforcing Positive Behavior in Children

One of the toughest yet the most rewarding part of parenting is the reinforcement of positive behavior in children. Reinforcement of positive behavior not only helps your children become better individuals growing up, but it also allows them to avoid or manage the potential problems that might await them down the road. This is where the idea of celebrating small wins can be a game-changer.

Positive reinforcement helps encourage prosocial behaviors such as following directions or sharing, while preventing unfavorable behaviors like spitting, hitting and violating rules. It also makes children more responsible, which ushers them to doing chores, doing homework, or getting along with their siblings and peers.

If you are a parent who wants to reinforce positive behavior in children, there are a few things you must ensure. These things include consistency, limit-setting, kindness, and encouragement. Essentially, when you offer a reward to your children for behaving well, it motivates them and encourages them to keep behaving the same way going forward.

For example, a person goes to work every day, so he or she may receive a paycheck toward the end of the month. While there are other aspects to sound professional performance, like recognition and a sense of self-actualization, a paycheck is their primary motivation.

Children are no different. When they see you celebrating and reinforcing certain behaviors, they are more likely to repeat them to the point where such behaviors become part of their overall demeanor.

Contrary to popular belief, in order to reinforce positive behaviors in children you don't need to spend.

It would be an added advantage if you did, but it isn't mandatory. However, some simple gestures of celebration can come in just as handy. Here are a few examples.

- A high five

- A thumbs up

- Giving them a hug

- Giving them a pat on the back.

- Offering to indulge in a fun activity like a board game with them.

- A few simple words of praise.

- Sharing your child's wins with other people, and making sure they are aware of it.

That said, you can multiply the praise and encouragement with something more tangible like a surprise gift. Suppose your child helps you clean the room or do the dishes after a family meetup. In order to appreciate their behavior, you can get them the toy car they have been asking you for.

Remember, you must appreciate your children for their progress and their improvement. Do not expect them to be perfect, or you will overwhelm them, and they will resort to behaving differently from what you expect of them.

Suppose you assigned the task of cleaning the living room to your child, and somehow, they forgot their bag on the couch. Rather than criticizing this small slip-up, you must appreciate them for their efforts. Similarly, you might have asked them to go to the bathroom to brush their teeth before bed, but they got distracted on the way. This can be frustrating but do not yell or scold. Instead, gently remind them of what you had asked them to do.

In addition, try to appreciate the very moment a positive behavior starts. For example, your child is weak in math, and would avoid the math homework until one day they try to give it a shot independently. Make them realize you have noticed this change in their behavior, and how happy it makes you.

Here are a few behaviors you must reinforce as a parent.

- Being friendly

- Taking an interest in physical activities

- Completing house chores, or at least trying

- Being flexible

- Complying with your requests

- Listening to disagreements without throwing a hissy fit

- Helping you without you even asking for it

- Playing peacefully with their siblings and other children

- Making an effort to complete a difficult task

- Being compassionate

- Not being restless

- Expressing their feelings

- Being well-mannered

- Being patient

If you can revisit the paragraphs above, we spoke about consistency from the parents' end. Think of a professional setting. A person goes to work for the paycheck, performance recognition, and periodic appraisals. Suppose your boss offers you a decent appraisal and completely forgets about it in the next cycle. You would instantly think about bouncing and would start looking for better opportunities.

The same basic principle applies to children. If you praise them occasionally or as per your convenience, their behaviors are unlikely to change. Remember, you don't have to offer your child a reward every time, either. However, for younger kids, the more you appreciate positive behavior, the better. There has to be a balance between positively reinforcing their behaviors and bribing them into eliciting a certain behavior from them.

The goal here is to make the child realize that their positive behavior makes good things happen. For example, if your child helps you prepare dinner, you can let them decide the menu for Christmas. Similarly, if they share their toys with their siblings and friends, you can let them play a little longer before going to bed.

In some cases, you can also allow your child to choose the reward for themselves. This will give them a sure-shot source of motivation, thus enhancing the likelihood of them following the desired behavior as they go forth.

Lastly, it is important to realize that parents should not offer accidental positive reinforcement in the case of negative behaviors. Sometimes, in order to get the attention they need, children engage in negative behaviors. Try to avoid these behaviors rather than coming up with things like "Stop that" or "Cut it out."

Another way parents reinforce negative behavior is by giving in. Be very clear about how you want your child to behave. By knowing exactly what you want, you will find it easier to reinforce their behaviors.

Celebrating your child's wins and milestones, regardless of how big or small they are is an important part of parenting. It gives them a sense of accomplishment, makes them persevere in the face of difficulty, and it also reinforces positive behavior. When you acknowledge their efforts, and celebrate their wins, you end up laying a strong foundation for your child's future. When children are appreciated, they tend to develop a growth mindset, which helps them become stronger and more confident individuals when they grow up, and it also gives them a sense of belongingness.

Chapter 15: Addressing Challenges

We've finally reached the end of this book! It's been a journey for all of us—you, the amazing readers, and me, the author. Writing this book made me revisit different aspects of parenthood and reflect on how they apply to the world we live in today.

This chapter is a bit different. Instead of specific tips and tricks, we'll discuss some of the most common challenges parents face today.

While there is nothing more rewarding and fulfilling than raising a child you love and adore and vice versa, the process can be arduously overwhelming, considering the sheer number of challenges it presents. Sure, brushing these parenting challenges under the rug is very tempting, but it's certainly not the best thing to do. Let's explore why it is important to address parenting issues head-on.

To begin with, unaddressed issues have a snowball effect. Suppose your child throws a hissy fit in public, which can make things embarrassing for you. You have two choices before you. You can either address the problem at hand or avoid it to enjoy a few minutes of peace. The intelligent thing to do would be to identify the root of the problem. If you fail to do so, the child may develop serious behavioral problems, and things may get out of hand going forward.

Moreover, you might stay oblivious to the difficulties facing your child. For example, your child might be struggling with homework. If you avoid the issue, you will never realize why they are struggling with homework in the first place. Do they need more guidance with a specific course, or is the house too noisy for them, or are there any distractions keeping them from focusing on their homework? Troubleshooting any of these reasons might eliminate the problem altogether.

Avoiding parenting issues may also result in a negative emotional impact. Suppose you get the feeling that your child is being bullied at school. You think that avoiding the conversation protects their emotions, whereas, in reality, it is the polar opposite of what you think. Your avoidance of the problem at hand can make them feel alone and less cared for, thus making them completely unable to cope with the problem. By addressing the issue effectively, you will be doing your child a major service.

Sometimes, avoiding these issues can result in long-term behavioral problems in children. Suppose your child has started lying to avoid getting into trouble. As a parent, it isn't hard to tell when a child is lying. Either you can sweep it under the carpet, or you can confront them. Confrontation doesn't mean being angry with them, either. If you fail to address the problem, the child may become dishonest as he grows old and might lie more often to avoid accountability. Moreover, addressing such issues will also help you build trust with your child.

The worst part is that avoiding potential inconveniences keeps you and your children from developing a healthy bond, and you both miss out on some amazing bonding opportunities. Suppose you and your teenager have been having too many arguments lately. You can totally avoid these altercations, but it's not something you would want to do. Instead, it might create distance between the two of you. On the flip side, addressing the issue might help you and your child understand each other's perspectives. You might even find a common ground, which will strengthen your bond.

Speaking of parenting challenges faced by parents, one of the biggest issues is teaching patience to your children. Patience is indeed a virtue, but in modern times, it has become annoyingly difficult for parents to impart this noble characteristic to their children. Part of it concerns the overt use of gadgets in the hands of little children.

With the internet, social media, and video streaming platforms like YouTube, children have gotten used to getting things with a singular click. Interestingly, the physical world doesn't play by the same rules as the digital realm, and in order to get what you want, you have to wait.

Here are some basic obstacles that prevent parents from raising more patient children.

Brain Development

Sometimes, the difficulties parents face when trying to teach patience to their children are not due to extraneous variables. Instead, they can be completely internal and, in this case, physical. The human brain is home to two different areas known as the prefrontal cortex and the limbic system. The former is responsible for helping people make plans, choices, and decisions for the future and is, therefore, more rational. The prefrontal cortex of a child takes time to develop, and therefore, it is difficult for them to grasp ideas like waiting or delayed gratification.

Less Understanding of Time

It is a fact that younger children don't have a stronger grasp on the idea of time. This is one of the reasons why five minutes to them can seem like an eternity to them. On top of that, when you try to teach them time with words like "soon," "yet," or "later," things can become frustrating for them. In this case, it is up to the parents to be patient enough so their children may learn patience.

The World That Exists Today

As I mentioned in the beginning, the world we live in is becoming increasingly impatient. Because of the rampant infiltration of the internet in our lives, the population in general has become impatient. From watching Netflix and ordering food to buying groceries online, everything happens with a single click, which makes people, especially children, get used to instant gratification. As for children, such a culture makes the idea of waiting and being patient irrelevant and unreasonable.

Difficulty With Emotions

It is difficult for children to manage their emotions, and it takes some time before they can learn to manage how they feel and how they choose to express it. Until then, they are most likely to yell, scream, shout, cry, or throw a temper tantrum when they are overwhelmed and don't know much about being patient. This is one of the reasons why teaching them patience can often be a fruitless exercise.

Parents Are Also Impatient

A lot of the things children learn are the ones they see around them, and patience isn't an exception. Children are impressionable, and they tend to mirror the behaviors of their parents. Sadly, with time, the world has become annoyingly competitive, and in the process of fulfilling their responsibilities, patience is the last thing you can expect from the parents of today. When children observe their parents lashing out due to a lack of patience, they feel it is the only way to react.

Now, let's shift gears and talk about some simple but effective techniques to raise more patient children.

Start Slow

Ask your child to wait five minutes before tuning into their favorite show. It will be tough for them, and they might act up, but starting slow will gradually instill patience in them. Similarly, ask your child to stay calm and composed while you prepare them a snack. Start with five minutes, and slowly increase the waiting duration. As they get older, teach them to wait for longer durations before their needs and wants are fulfilled. In addition, you can use fun exercises like the word bubble. Ask your child to blow an imaginary word bubble and fill it up with everything they have to say while you talk over the phone. This way, they won't interrupt you while you listen to important phone calls.

Do Not Offer Instant Gratification

This is by far the most difficult one, but it will build a solid character for them as they grow older. So, the next time your child asks you to make them a sandwich, you can tell them you would love to do that, but they would have to wait for X number of minutes before you can finish an important task. Besides patience, such an approach will also teach them self-control. Once the decided period has elapsed, you can give them what you want. By doing so, you will teach them their wishes will be granted if they choose to stay calm. Do not give in if your child acts up.

Leverage the Power of Games

Sometimes, toddlers can have a hard time being patient. This is where games can come in handy, but not just any game. Games that come in handy are the way to go in this case. Family-friendly indoor games like Connect-Four or Candy-Land are some perfect game options to teach your child how to wait. As you play, say things like, "It's my turn now. You will have to wait for yours."

Give Them a Positive Experience

Do not make the mistake of turning the whole waiting exercise into a punishment. Do not get angry if your child asks if the wait is over. It is totally natural, and they are most likely to ask. It is because they don't have the ability to conceptualize time yet. By staying calm during the whole exercise, you will eventually make it a healthy and positive experience for them.

Problem-Solving Strategies

As a parent, you cannot eliminate the problems you will experience while raising children. How you react in the process will affect your child and play a crucial part in transforming them into the kind of people they will become. Suppose you are having difficulty raising kids, and the problems are too overwhelming for you. In that case, I have put together some simple but effective strategies for you so you may easily solve these problems.

Define the Problem

- Try to determine what's happening, when it's happening, and who is responsible. For example, you and your child have been arguing a lot. Try to figure out how often it happens and who initiates it.

- Try to focus on the problem more than the person doing it. Figure out why there are so many arguments in the first place.

- Take full ownership of the part you play in these arguments.

- Adopt a neutral and non-blaming approach.

What Do Each of You Want?

- What do you both want or need?

- Are you both concerned or afraid of something?

- What is it that you don't want or need?

Come Up with Solutions/Brainstorm

- Take turns and put forth ideas one by one.

- Encourage your child to share ideas, even if their ideas seem irrelevant or unreasonable.

- Rejecting ideas can offend or potentially hurt your child.

- Make sure to get enough ideas before you sit down to talk about them.

Evaluate Solutions

- Cross off ideas you both know won't work.

- List down the merits and demerits of each and every idea. There has to be something positive about each idea.

- Cross off ideas that have more demerits than merits.

- Rate the remaining ideas on a scale from one to 10.

Review the Solutions

This is where you need to step up as a parent, for this part requires some analytical work your kids might not be capable of, especially if they are younger than the pubescent age. Here is what you will do.

- Find out if the solution is working.

- What has worked and what hasn't?

- What can be done to make things work smoothly?

Remember, if your children are under ten years of age, do not be too intellectual or philosophical with this exercise. Instead, keep it fun and light-hearted, and use lingo that is understandable for your children and doesn't overwhelm or bore them.

As a parent, it is very tempting to avoid some of the hard-hitting issues, but it is something that must be done. Not only does it make things easier for you going forward, but it also helps you raise more sorted and enterprising members of society who are up-standing and morally sound. In addition, make sure to teach your children the importance of being patient. In order to do so, make sure they don't get instant gratification. Lastly, if you are having issues with your children, talk to them about it, and don't forget to include them when you evaluate solutions.

Remember, parenting is a beautiful, messy, ever-evolving adventure. There will be triumphs and tears, sleepless nights, and moments of pure joy. While this book has equipped you with tools and knowledge, you already possess the most important ingredient: love. Trust your instincts, embrace the journey, and know that even the most seasoned parents learn something new every day. You've got this!

www.ingramcontent.com/pod-product-compliance
Lightning Source LLC
Chambersburg PA
CBHW060859140726

47996CB00001B/44